# CHARLIE & ME

"The only things in life that are permanent
are memories."
-- Charles Bronson

**Also by Harriett Bronson**

*Shut Up, I'm on the Phone*
*Do I Have a House for You!*

A. Memoir

# CHARLIE & ME

Harriett Bronson

Timberlake
p r e s s

www.TimberlakePress.com

First Printing 2011

Although the author and publisher have made every effort to ensure the accuracy and completeness of information contained in this book, we assume no responsibility for errors, inaccuracies, omissions, or any inconsistencies herein. Any slights of people, places or organizations are unintentional.

Library of Congress cataloging-in-Publications Data

ISBN 978-0-9828847-0-6
Printed in United States of America

For information contact:
Timberlake Press
Box 129
Woodland Hills, CA 91365
www.TimberlakePress.com

Cover photo: Fred Hess & Son, Atlantic City, N.J.
Back cover photo: Sylvia Cary

This book is dedicated

To my children, Suzanne and Tony, who will hopefully understand the "why" of things that happened in our lives;

And to my editor, Sylvia Cary, without whose generosity and help this story would never have been written.

# Acknowledgments

My heartfelt thanks to the men who helped put
my life back together and regain my sanity:

Ron & Fred Beaton
Buddy Garion
Joe Mullins
Steven Peck
Regis Philbin
Jim Simon
Larry Sloan
Simon Taub

And to my loyal and dear girlfriends who
have always been supportive and "there" for me
and helped me keep my boat afloat.

# Contents

# Chapter 1
## Love at the Bessie V. Hicks School
## of Stage, Screen and Radio

"C'mere."

I couldn't believe he was speaking to me. Nobody had ever talked to me that crudely. I was standing at the water fountain at the top of the stairs of the Bessie V. Hicks School of Stage, Screen and Radio in Philadelphia. It was my second day.

I dabbed my lips with the back of my hand: "What?"

"C'mere!" he said again, looking right at me with brown eyes set in a wonderfully intense face. His dark hair was slicked back in a duck tail and he was wearing a gray sharkskin zoot suit.

Then, as though being reeled in, I went over and stood in front of him.

"You have the prettiest mouth I've ever seen," he said.

I was flummoxed but managed a reply: "Thank you."

He grinned. "What's your name?"

"Harriett Tendler."

He didn't offer his name in return. I had to know. "What's yours?"

"Charlie Buchinsky."

"Are you a student here?"

"Why do you ask that?"

"You look older."

"G.I. bill."

He glanced down the hallway where two other students, Honey and Beth, were waiting for me. "How come you girls always travel in packs?"

"They're my friends."

"Shake `em. Have coffee with me at Child's."

I was shocked. "I can't."

"Why not?"

"I have class."

"Bye, then."

With a curt little wave, he headed down the stairs and out the double glass doors to the street.

I joined Honey and Beth and we walked into class together.

"Who was that?" Honey asked.

"He looks like a killer," Beth added dramatically. "He gives me the willies."

"He asked me out for coffee."

Honey didn't wait a beat. "You're not going to go!"

"Of course not."

And so began my love story with Charlie Buchinsky, aka Charles Bronson. The year was 1947. I had just turned eighteen; Charlie was twenty-six. We were to be together for the next eighteen years -- and in each other's lives for a total of fifty-six years until his death on August 30, 2003.

We were a most unlikely couple -- Charlie, one of eleven children (one died) born to an immigrant Lithuanian, Catholic coal miner and his wife, and I, the only child of a widowed Jewish cattle breeder and dairy farmer. I was on my way (or so I fancied) to an acting career on the New York stage when Charlie uttered that magic word to me -- "C'mere" -- and sent my life off in another direction.

The only thing Charlie and I had in common was a stubborn (my father's word) determination to be together and to make Charlie into a movie star.

## Chapter 2
### Helen Hayes, Move Over

I loved drama school. Every day when I walked up the steps and read the sign over the entrance, *Bessie V. Hicks School of Stage, Screen and Radio*, I'd feel a thrill. It had been a struggle to get there. Ever since I'd had the lead in my high school play, *Junior Miss*, I knew acting was in my future. I could taste it.

My father had fought me every step of the way.

"You're not going!" Sam Tendler shouted the first time I told him I wanted to go to drama school.

"Daddy, I'm going."

"You should go to business school. A woman should know how to work."

"I'm going to be a star on the Broadway stage and marry a rich man and have servants."

I heard him sigh and mutter under his breath, "What am I going to do with this girl?" Then louder, "Harriett, why can't you just settle down instead of wanting what you can't have?"

Next came the inevitable: "You're as stubborn as your mother. It killed her and it'll kill you, too."

I knew what was at the root of Sam Tendler's tirades. It was fear. I was all he had and he was afraid of losing me. He was afraid I would disappear into "Life" and something terrible would happen to me because that's what happened to my mother.

My mother, Frances, had had a passion for riding horses, a passion my father not only didn't share, but hated. Every photograph I have of her shows her in jodhpurs. Apparently her determination to ride was so great that my father finally realized he was powerless over it. He gave up trying to dissuade her.

It was a decision he later came to regret.

One day when my mother went horseback riding in Fairmont Park in Philadelphia, her horse ran away with her, threw her and she hit her head against a tree. It killed her.

She was twenty-eight years old. I was not yet three.

I don't remember my mother, at least not consciously. But I don't think it's a coincidence that all my life I've been terrified that the people I love will walk out the door and never come back.

After my mother's death I was sent to live with her family in their big house in West Philadelphia. There was my grandmother, Gram Katie Fenkel, my aunt Sophye Fenkel (my mother's sister) and my handsome young uncles, Steve and Morris.

Every Sunday my father would come to visit me. I'd sit on his lap and he'd open his pocket watch and show me a picture of *me*, which I loved. Then he'd take me to a show. It was Stanley (some say he preferred "Stan Lee") Broza's *Horn and Hardart's Children's Hour* radio show, broadcast live with an audience. I'd stand on my seat to see and hear every single minute of it. Afterwards, my father would take me back to my grandmother's house. That was our weekly routine.

The minute he'd drop me off and leave, I'd get a stomach ache, afraid I'd never see him again. When I was married to Charlie the same thing would happen when he'd go off on location -- I'd get stomach aches.

As a child, I remember crying a lot. I was skinny and wouldn't eat, which worried everybody. My beautiful Aunt Sophye, who doted on me, was always weighing me. I was fascinated by her. I loved watching her dress up in long gowns when she went out on dates. I'd clomp around after her in her shoes, decked out in jewelry that used to be my mother's, and I'd pretend that I was going out on a date, too.

Later on, when I was older, I was told that it was during this period that my father had been briefly remarried. When his bride wanted him to send me away to a boarding school, he refused and they were divorced.

During the first week of drama school I was in a play-reading class. Paired with a male student, we stood at the front of the class and read a scene from Chekhov's *The Sea Gull*. The drama teacher stood nearby, following along. I read the role of Masha and my partner read the role of Medvedenko.

Wearing an ankle-length "new look" plaid skirt and cashmere sweater set, with my long dark hair tied back into a pony tail, I was aware that every boy in the room was watching me.

One of them was Charlie Buchinsky.

"In *The Sea Gull* there's a play within a play," the drama teacher said. "It's tricky. 'Medvedenko,' you're up first."

MEDVEDENKO turns to MASHA:

MEDVEDENKO: *Why do you always wear black?*

MASHA: *I am in mourning for my life. I am unhappy. But come, the play is just about to begin.*

I remember noticing that I wasn't the least bit nervous or self-conscious. I loved it. I glanced over at Charlie. He winked. Embarrassed, I looked away.

MEDVEDENKO: *This play always makes me sad.*

MASHA: *Why is that?*

MEDVEDENKO: *Because it's about a boy and a girl who are in love with each other -- just as I am in love with you -- but in real life you don't return my love so I am wretched.*

"Sound wretched then, don't whine!" the drama teacher shouted at my partner.

MEDVEDENKO: *Every day I walk four miles to get here just to see you, but when I arrive I am met with indifference. But I cannot blame you. The truth is, I am a man without means. Who would want to marry a man who hasn't a penny?*

MASHA: *It isn't money that matters, Medvedenko. A poor man may be happy –*

The drama teacher jumped in again. "Harriett, don't be so nice here. Sound a little more impatient with this guy. He's trying to make you feel guilty for not loving him."

I could see Charlie a few rows back, his eyes riveted on me. A few seats away from him was his pal, Joe Roman, who, I was to learn later, had actually been the one responsible for Charlie's presence at Bessie V. Hicks. Prior to that, Charlie had been enrolled at the Hession School of Art. When he'd first applied to drama school, Bessie Hicks, the head of the school, had been so unnerved by his looks that she didn't want to admit him until Joe Roman vouched for him.

Joe quickly picked up on Charlie's interest in me. "The cashmere sweater girl's not from South Philly, Charlie, so forget about it," he said to Charlie in a loud whisper, loud enough for me to hear.

Charlie smirked. "That's what I like."

I went on as though I'd heard nothing.

MASHA: *Your love touches me, Medvedenko, but I cannot reciprocate it.*

"Much better," I heard the drama teacher say.

MASHA: *How stifling it is in here!*

The drama teacher interrupted again: "Hit the word 'stifling' because what you're feeling is that this man wants to possess you."

MASHA: *How stifling it is in here!*

Automatically, my hands went up to my throat. I moved to the classroom window, pretended to open it for air.
"That's good," the drama teacher said.

MASHA: *There must be a storm coming, Medvedenko. You really must leave before it pours. Quickly, go! Go!*

My reading partner exited stage right, looking back at me with a miserable expression on his face.
The class applauded as we took our bows, both of us smiling. We returned to our seats.

"Helen Hayes move over!" Honey gushed to me on the way out of the classroom. I could feel Charlie's eyes drilling into the back of my head.
"Quick, he's following us. Let's get out of here!" I said.
Honey and I broke into a run – down the stairs, out the double glass doors, down the front steps and down Chestnut Street to the subway.
Safe!

## Chapter 3
## Sam Tendler

Two and a half years after my mother had died – when I was four -- my father bought a dairy farm and took me to live with him. It was called "Cinchona Farm."

We had a housekeeper who watched over me while my father worked. I kept her busy. I think I had every childhood disease. My father never took me to a doctor. This wasn't for religious reasons; he simply didn't believe in doctors. He had the school nurse come to the farm to see me instead.

Along with dairy farming, my father became a breeder of Guernsey cows. He named a calf after me and I was given the responsibility of feeding it every morning before school. I used to get up at five to accompany him as he delivered milk to nearby estates. In warm weather, we'd take Sunday drives to various farms for ice cream. He'd whistle while we drove.

It was unusual for Jewish people to live in that part of Pennsylvania, let alone own farms -- and even more unusual for a widowed father to raise his daughter alone. Sam Tendler looked like Spencer Tracy. He had thick auburn hair and women were always after him. Without fail they'd remark, "Isn't it a shame, Sam, that Harriett doesn't have your red hair." For the most part, my father's lady friends catered to me, wanting to win me over. I liked that.

Life on the farm was lonely, not just because it was somewhat isolated, but because of religious prejudice. Throughout my school years, I was always the only Jewish student. In grammar school, a classmate once put a snake down my back and called me "a dirty Jew." In junior high school and high school, I was never invited to join after-school activities, nor was I invited by any of my classmate to be their friend outside of school. However, I took it upon myself to become involved in activities *inside* school, and my father made it a point to involve me in a synagogue where I was "confirmed" at age sixteen. I made friends through the synagogue. Unfortunately, it was far from the farm so in order to see my new friends, I had to walk a mile, then take a bus, then a trolley into Philadelphia -- and back.

For the most part, things went well on the farm up until 1943 when my father sold a heifer to another farm -- and even though he had always had our cows tested -- it was discovered that the heifer had Bangs disease, an infectious disease of cattle. Ultimately, his entire herd of cows was wiped out and he had to give up that part of his business life.

After that, he became depressed. I loved him dearly, but when I saw my strong, secure father becoming morose, not only did it frighten me, it angered me. Suddenly, he wanted to sell the farm and get out of there. I was then fourteen (we were in the middle of World War II) and I begged him not to move because I wanted to complete high school with my class. We stayed, but the housekeeper left and I kept house. And his depression got even worse. It went on for years. It didn't lift until long after I'd left home to get married to Charlie, and my father had married a big blond named Ann. That did the trick.

His remarriage, along with his improved mood, was a big relief to me since I'd always felt so guilty for abandoning him.

## Chapter 4
## Radio Days

My companion in my loneliness on the farm was my radio. Next to the theatre, I loved the radio. It was a great comfort and I almost believed that everyone on the radio was talking directly to me. Oddly enough, even when I was in drama school, the idea of "radio" as a career never occurred to me. My interest then was in being a stage actress, not in being a "radio actress."

I listened to *Orson Wells* and *Arch Oboler* and all the comedy shows -- *Jack Benny; Fibber Magee and Molly; Bob Hope,* and *Joe Penner.* The one radio show I most looked forward to every Saturday night was *Your Hit Parade* with Frank Sinatra. I loved Frank Sinatra. He was my first crush. Posters of him were plastered on the walls of my bedroom, along with playbills from Broadway shows and signed glossy photos of Tyrone Power, Errol Flynn, John Garfield and, of course, Sinatra.

Years later, when Charlie worked on a movie with Steve McQueen and Frank Sinatra, I finally met him. Charlie made me promise not to tell him that I had been one of those "bobby soxers" who had a crush on him. I ended up writing a short story about my adventures as a fifteen-year-old trying to meet Sinatra called *"Out for Stars."* It was published many years later (the early 1980's) in the Sunday *Los Angeles Times.*

In 1947, soon after I had graduated from Springfield Township High School, we finally made the move back into Philadelphia. I was thrilled to be able to walk only five blocks to visit my friend, Elaine. I came to appreciate not being isolated from people. To this day, friendships are important to me and I don't take them for granted.

My father's deep depression (he hadn't yet met Ann) continued to hover over the household like a cloud, making it increasingly hard to be around him. He was either fighting me, or he was sitting in a chair being sad.

Most afternoons I'd go to Child's Restaurant next door to the school, or to the library, or to my Aunt Sophye's dress shop -- anyplace so I didn't have to go home until the very last minute. When I couldn't delay it any longer, I'd finally get on the subway, get off at the Germantown stop, walk to the corner of Washington Lane and Chew Street and then drag myself up the nearly two dozen narrow steps that led to our front door.

I'd usually find Sam Tendler sitting in the dark.

"Daddy, why do you do this? Turn on a light so you can see."

He'd sigh: "There's nothing I want to see."

Irritated, I'd go around the apartment turning on lights. "What would you do if I didn't come home one night, just sit here until morning?"

"You always come home."

"But what if I didn't?"

"You always do."

I'd give up. "You want to go see a movie?"

"You and your movies. No movie."

"Aren't you going to ask me how I like drama school?"

"Aren't you going to ask me how I like throwing my money down the drain?"

"You're investing in my future. I love drama school, by the way. I'm so grateful you're sending me there."

"I'm probably making a big mistake. A big mistake."

"Why don't I fix you something to eat?"

His answer was always the same: "I'm not hungry."

"You're never hungry. You'll get sick."

He'd sigh again.

"I'll fix you something anyway."

By the time I'd put food in front of him, I was usually so exasperated I'd escape to my room to listen to the radio.

On the days I came home from school earlier, I'd listen to soap operas. When it was time for *Helen Trent*, I'd lie down on my bed, gaze up at my playbills from Broadway shows and my collection of autographed photos of movie stars, and daydream about my fabulous future:

ANNOUNCER: *The real-life drama of Helen Trent who -- when life mocks her, breaks her hopes, dashes her against the rocks of despair -- fights back bravely, successfully, to prove what so many women long to prove in their own lives -- that because a woman is thirty-five or more, romance in life need not be over, that romance can begin at thirty-five.*

I knew that, unlike Helen Trent, when *I* was thirty-five my life would be perfect. I'd be a famous Broadway actress. I'd be happily married to a great actor like John Garfield and I'd have half a dozen children. Furthermore, unlike my mother, I'd *live* to raise them. And, unlike my father, I wouldn't be depressed when I was around them. My father would be proud of me and see that sending me to drama school was the best decision he'd ever made. And my classmates who'd shunned me would be sorry.

As it turned out, the year I turned thirty-five was the year I lost Charlie, which was followed by years of depression -- just like my father.

## Chapter 5
### I Can See Your Face up on That Silver Screen

I was late to school. I'd been doing chores around the apartment to placate my father, and now I was going to be a few minutes late to my play-reading class. I arrived at Bessie V. Hicks out of breath from running from the subway stop. All the students were in class except for one -- Charlie.

He was waiting for me outside the classroom door, leaning against the wall, arms folded, a smirk on his face.

"You're late," he said.

"No kidding."

"Punctuality is a virtue."

I had been looking forward to reading the part of Blanche DuBois in *A Streetcar Named Desire.*

"They've already picked a Blanche," Charlie said, reading my mind.

"What about her sister?"

"Her sister, too. Let's go to Child's for coffee."

"I don't drink coffee."

"There's a first time for everything. C'mon."

There was no saying no to him. I couldn't even think of the word. When he started to walk down the hall, I followed.

Child's was a gothic-looking place with a high, vaulted ceiling. Since it was next door to Bessie V. Hicks, it was usually jammed with students, but because we were playing hooky it was nearly deserted. Charlie guided me to a booth and ordered coffee.

"What if I don't like it?"

"You won't know until you try it. Tell me something, do you always worry about things in advance?"

I shrugged.

"Charlie Chan say, 'He who worries in advance gets to experience it twice.'"

I couldn't help it -- I laughed.

The waitress brought us the coffee.

Charlie reached for the cream. "Put cream in it."

Obediently, I poured some in.

"Put sugar in it."

I put sugar in it. I tasted it. "It's okay," I said politely.

"You're lying," Charlie said. "Don't ever do that"

"All right then, I hate it."

"You'll get used to it."

"Are you from Philadelphia?" I asked.

"Scooptown."

"What's Scooptown?"

"Coal mining town."

"And you're from there?"

"Yeah, why not?"

"What's its real name?"

"You sure ask a lot of questions."

"I like to know things," I said.

"What else you wanna know?"

"What was it like being in the war? Was it awful?"

"Best deal I ever had. Slept good. Ate good."

"You're the first person I've ever heard say nice things about the army."

"You're going to hear me say a lot of things you never heard anyone say."

"Assuming we have another conversation after this one."

"We will."

"We'll see about that."

Some students began to straggle in from the drama school.

"Let's take a walk," Charlie said. "It's like Grand Central Station in here."

"There's seven or eight people."

"Seven or eight too many."

During a stroll through the Navy Yard I kept sneaking little glances at Charlie.

"Anybody ever tell you you look like John Garfield?"

"Nope."

"I saw *Body and Soul* five times."

"You paid for it five times?"

"I did."

"Sucker."

"Did you ever think about acting in the movies?" I asked.

"More questions. Nope."

"I get these pictures in my mind's eye sometimes, so clear it's like it's already happened. Sometimes they come true."

"Mind's eye?"

"In my imagination. In my mind's eye I can see your face up on the silver screen."

"*This* puss? You're nuts."

"Why do you want to be an actor?"

"You oughta work for the FBI."

"Is it the intimacy of having the audience right there in the same space with you? Is it the ability to vary each performance and perfect it?"

Charlie stopped in his tracks.

"You wanna know why I want to be an actor?"

I nodded.

He reached into his pocket, withdrew his hand and opened it. There were four pennies sitting in the middle of his palm. "That's until payday."

He put the pennies back. We resumed walking.

"That guy in class, Joe Roman. He got me free tickets to a play once. *Anna Lucasta.* You know how much actors make?"

"How much?"

"Sixty-five bucks."

"A week?"

"A performance. Hell, that ain't even work. People who think acting's hard don't have coal mining to compare it to."

I mulled over the idea that someone would want to become an actor just for the money. It seemed wrong.

"There's more to life than making money. You want to know why I want to be an actress?"

"I'll bite."

"Because I love it. So much I'd do it for free."

"You better marry a rich man."

I tossed my head. "I intend to."

"And you better learn to act."

That was a punch in the gut. "You don't think I can act?"

"I could tell you were acting."

"I *was* acting."

"*'Acting's okay, just don't let them catch you doing it.'* I heard a guy say that on the radio once."

"You've been in drama school *how* long? A *week*? And now you're an expert?"

Charlie took the end of my long, dark brown wool scarf and held it up to my face.

"You oughta wear more brown. It brings out your eyes."

I melted.

"We'll have coffee again." He gave me a tender kiss on the top of my head and sent me on my way.

I glided down the subway steps as though in a dream.


At home that night I ripped through my closet and pulled out everything I owned that was brown. "Brown, brown, where are you brown?" I sang to myself as I found items and held them up to the mirror. I chose a brown cashmere sweater to wear to drama school the very next day.

## Chapter 6
## Pasta Perfect

Charlie and I began seeing each other. Most of the time I paid for our coffee dates because Charlie never had any money. That was not an issue for either one of us. I didn't tell anybody I was seeing him. I'd just disappear after school or I'd skip school altogether.

"Where have you *been* lately?" Honey demanded.

"Nowhere special. Home with my father or at Aunt Sophye's dress shop."

"I don't believe you. I bet you've been seeing that guy who looks dangerous."

"He's not dangerous. He's nice."

"Ah-ha!"

No matter what time I got home, I'd find my father sitting in the dark, waiting for me. He'd grill me.

"You're late."

"I went out for coffee after school."

"You don't drink coffee."

"I'm learning."

"Who with?" he demanded.

"Just a friend from school."

"What friend?"

"Nobody you know, Daddy."

I'd try to distract him. "I went to see Aunt Sophye and Gram Katie at the dress shop the other day. They said I can have a job there any time I want."

He glanced over at a picture of my mother in her jodhpurs. "I wish your mother were here." Deep sigh. "If you were seeing somebody you'd tell me, right?

"Come on, Daddy, stop cross-examining me."

Three nights a week Charlie worked at Freihoffer's Bakery, sorting rolls.

"I get paid Friday," he told me a week or so after we'd started dating. "I wanna take you someplace to eat. My treat."

"A real restaurant?"

"Yeah, a real restaurant!" he said, a little defensively. "What, you think guys from South Philly don't go to real restaurants?"

"That's not what I meant! I meant I want to know what to wear."

"Dress up, of course. What do you *think*?"

The restaurant was Victor's Italian on Catherine Street. Here, Charlie was already a star. He knew everybody. The owner, Leon, greeted him warmly, as did the waiters, the bartenders, the patrons.

"So this is the uptown girl you've been bragging about, Charlie! Pretty soon you'll be too good for South Philly."

Leon led us to a prime table near a small stage where opera students were taking turns singing operatic selections or playing old Caruso records over the loudspeaker.

He snapped open two huge white linen napkins and placed them on our laps.

"The usual?" Leon asked.

Charlie nodded, and Leon headed off for the kitchen.

"How do you know all these people?" I asked.

"A lot of 'em go to my gym."

A waiter appeared with two huge plates of spaghetti and meatballs, followed by another waiter with a basket of hot garlic bread. Hungrily, we plunged in. I looked up and saw Charlie artfully twisting his spaghetti on his fork. I was impressed

"How do you know how to do that?"

"Do what?"

"Twist your spaghetti like that?"

Charlie looked at me deadpan: "Finishing school."

I laughed aloud and nearly choked on my garlic bread.

Charlie signaled for the owner's attention. "Let's have a spotlight over here!" Suddenly, a bright stage spot was on our table.

Then, in the glare of the spot, in full view of everyone in the restaurant, Charlie leaned over and kissed me full on the lips.

The waiters, opera students and customers went crazy.

"Bravo! Charlie! Bravo!" and then, "Encore! Encore!"

My face was as red as the spaghetti sauce. And my heart was pounding.

Later, Charlie escorted me home on the subway. We were so busy kissing we missed the Germantown stop and had to do the whole circuit again.

When we arrived at my stop the second time he walked me halfway down the block. I stopped him. I didn't want him to walk me any further.

"Just in case my father is watching for me out the window," I said.

"Have dinner with me again next Friday," Charlie said.

"Victor's Italian?"

He shook his head. "My place."

I felt shocked. And I didn't say boo.

# Chapter 7
## Emily Street

A week later I was trotting down Emily Street in South Philly, right behind Charlie, helping him carry groceries. We passed a dozen row houses before we got to his rooming house. We walked up the front steps, in through the front door and mounted a flight of dingy stairs to Charlie's door.

Charlie's room was spare, neat, with a narrow bed made so tight you could bounce a quarter on it. A double hot-plate sat on a card table. There was a small sink. In a corner was an artist's easel with a canvas. Other canvases were leaning up against the wall. On the floor, barbells.

"Everything's so neat," I said.

"I like things neat." Charlie started unpacking the groceries.

I began nosing around the room. I stopped in front of the easel and studied the painting in progress which depicted a young man in a wooden tub being given a bath by an older woman.

"You didn't tell me you paint."

"You think a person should tell everything?"

"You have talent."

"That and ten cents will buy you a cup of coffee."

"Who's the painting of?"

"My mother and me."

He cut up potatoes as I flipped through the paintings leaning against the wall. "Is this your father?"

"It's just a miner I know. My father died of black lung when I was ten."

"I'm sorry."

Charlie shrugged. "That's the way it goes."

"My mother died when I was almost three. I don't even remember her. Do you remember your father?"

"Just the fear of him."

"My mother fell off a horse."

"Was she in the circus?"

I looked over to see if he was serious. He was.

"She loved to ride," I went on. "Her horse tripped and fell and she hit her head on a tree. It killed her instantly."

"What can you do? Don't think about it."

Charlie unwrapped a steak and put it on a plate. "C'mere. I'll show you how to cook steak the way I like it."

I watched while Charlie took a sharp knife and began to cut the fat off the steak.

"Veins, too?" I asked.

"Veins, too."

He dropped the potatoes into the pot of boiling water. "Boiled only, never any other way."

I found myself listening intently, as though trying to commit the instructions to memory.

After dinner, while Charlie washed dishes, I continued to explore the room. I stopped in front of the barbells. "What are these things?" I asked him.

"What I work out with when I don't go to the gym. Here, I'll show you."

"You do that on purpose?"

"Every damn day. How much do you weigh?"

"130."

"That's what I figured. You should weigh 118 tops."

"Thanks for the compliment!"

"It's the truth"

"But you don't have to say it."

"People can always improve and be better. Here, I'll show you what I do."

Charlie pulled off his shirt and, bare-chested, he lifted the barbells over his head, and then released them to the floor. I was impressed with his beautiful build and embarrassed to be looking at it. There was an awkward silence.

"How'd you get that scar on your shoulder?"

"A little souvenir from the war. I was a tail-gunner on a B-29 over Japan."

"You got that from a real bullet?"

"Yup."

"Amazing."

"I was sure amazed when it happened."

Charlie, still bare-chested, pulled me close to him and gave me a lingering kiss.

"Are you a virgin?"

"Yes."

"That's nice. I like that."

"I'm glad you approve of something."

He picked me up and carried me over to his narrow, neatly made bed.

"Charlie, I don't know about this."

"Relax, Miss Worry Wart," he said kindly. "I know what to do."

Gently, he put me down on the bed, sat down next to me and slowly began to undress me. As though hypnotized, I watched his face intently, watched his every move, studying how he went about this business of seducing me, fascinated by it. When I was naked, he took off his slacks and lay down on top of me, kissing me. I put my arms around his neck and pulled him close. And we made love.

Afterwards, we lay in each other's arm. I felt just fine. When Charlie pulled himself up on his elbows to look at the clock, I tightened my grip. "Don't move. Don't get up. I want to lie here like this forever."

"It's late, Harriett. I'll walk you to the subway. I've still got shirts to iron.

"I'll iron them."

"Why would you do that?"

"Because I want to *do* something for you. I want to *wait* on you. I want to *serve* you. " I was laughing, kissing his chest, his neck, his face. "So you'll let me?"

"I like my shirts ironed a certain way -- no creases. Here, I'll show you"

Charlie led me over to his closet. It was a work of art. Meticulous. The shirts were hung up according to color; the pants pressed and neatly folded over hangers; the highly polished shoes were lined up like troops.

Charlie picked out a shirt and held it up. "This is how I like them done. On a shirt board."

"I can do that."

"You *are* nuts!" he said as he stuffed a pile of washed but un-ironed shirts into a gym bag and handed it over to me.

I think I'm falling in love, I said to myself.

# Chapter 8
## Aunt Sophye

Now that I was dating Charlie, I wanted to buy things – girly things. Pretty underwear. Make-up. Shoes. So I started working at Sophye's Dress Shop after school three days a week -- the same days Charlie was working at Freihoffer's Bakery.

Aunt Sophye, who'd fought to get my father to agree to pay my drama school tuition, got a vicarious kick out of my progress there. I always suspected she harbored a secret desire to be an actress herself, but she never owned up to it.

I bounced into the dress shop one day, gave Gram Katie, who was playing solitaire at a card table in the back, a kiss and went to help Aunt Sophye take garments left in the dressing rooms and replace them on the racks.

"You're in a good mood."

"Yup."

"How was play-reading class?"

"I ditched."

"Why would you do that?"

"I met somebody," I whispered conspiratorially. "We went out for coffee."

"Instead of class?" Her face was suddenly grim.

"Yes!" I said, still grinning happily.

"You ditched for some stupid boy?"

"He's not a boy. He's older. He's special."

Aunt Sophye gave a sharp little laugh. "They're all special in the beginning. Believe me, I know."

It was the first time I'd considered that those glamorous dates Aunt Sophye went out on, all dressed up in those beautiful gowns, might have had a downside to them. She was still single. And she was starting to sound bitter.

"Maybe you'd be married by now if you'd stop letting the family talk you out of people."

"The trouble is the family's usually right. What's his name?"

"Charlie."

"Charlie what?"

"Charlie Buchinsky."

"Is he Jewish?"

"I don't know yet." I lied. I did know. He wasn't.

"You better find out because if he's not Jewish you can forget about it. Here, put these blouses on the rack by the front door."

I said no more. I did as I was told.

# Chapter 9
## The Proposal

At home after school, instead of studying lines in plays, I was now ironing shirts.

One Sunday night while I was listening to Lux Radio Theatre, there was a knock on my bedroom door.

"How can you listen to that crap?" my father yelled.

I turned the radio down and quickly hid Charlie's shirts, but I forgot about the one that was hanging on my closet door.

My father stuck his head in. "What are you up to in here?"

"Ironing."

He spotted the man's shirt. "Who does *that* belong to?"

"Someone I know."

"Someone who?"

"Just someone at school that I'm doing a favor for."

"I have half a mind to call up Bessie Hicks and find out what's going on down at that school. I'm not paying for you to take in laundry!"

Sam Tendler was true to his word. The next day when I got to school, Bessie V. Hicks herself was standing outside her office at the top of the stairs. She watched me as I climbed the stairs and walked down the hall to my classroom. She disappeared back into her office.

When I sat down next to Charlie in our stage make-up class, I was feeling unnerved. We were scheduled to do "aging" make-up on each other.

"Today I'm gonna see what you'll look like when you're old so I can decide if I should marry you or not," Charlie said.

I was so distracted I could hardly pay attention to him. "I think my father must have called Bessie Hicks to find out who I'm dating because she was out there spying on me when I got here."

"Old bat. I'll go talk to her."

"No!"

A lipstick rolled off the table and hit the floor. I leaned down to retrieve it.

Charlie kept on talking to me. "So if you pass the aging test, will you marry me?"

I was scrambling for the lipstick, still only half listening.

I found the lipstick and stood back up. "No."

"Did you hear what I asked you?"

I repeated what I'd heard: "'Are you mad at me?'"

"I said, `Will you marry me?'"

I stared at him a moment, still thinking of Bessie Hick's prune face, then I said in a half-hearted way, "Okay."

"'*Okay*'? That's *it*? You think that was easy?"

Then it hit me. "Oh, Charlie! I'm sorry -- yes! Yes!"

He grinned his Charlie grin.

Then my mood clouded. "If we're engaged that means you're going to have to meet my family."

"So?"

"They're kind of opinionated."

"Yeah? Well, so am I."

## Chapter 10
### The Announcement

The family gathered at Gram Katie's house to meet the man I was dating. I hadn't told them yet that we were engaged.

Gram Katie dusted the heavy Russian pieces of furniture and polished the silver. Aunt Sophye set the table while Uncle Steve and Uncle Morris played cards in the living room.

Meanwhile, my father fretted and paced.

"Sam, you look solemn, like death," Gram Katie said to him, her Russian accent thick even after so many years in America.

"I should have made her go to business school," my father said more than once.

"Maybe you like this man, yes? You know our *sheine meydele* would not bring home man who is not good man, yes?"

My father refused to be comforted.

Aunt Sophye went over to the window. "They just got off the trolley."

My father and Gram Katie joined her and peered out.

"Oh-oh, Sam!" said Aunt Sophye. "What have we got here?"

All of my father's worst fears were instantly realized. "He looks like a gangster."

Aunt Sophye fanned the flames. "And look at that awful suit."

Gram Katie scolded them: "Sophye, Sam, please! He's our guest."

"Harriett's gone and lost her mind."

During dinner we all tried to be polite. I decided not to break the news about our engagement until the conversation had turned to a topic that would make an appropriate segue.

"Harriett tells us you're from Ehrenfeld, Mr. Buchinsky," said Aunt Sophye. "Isn't that a coal mining town?"

Charlie confirmed her suspicion without a moment of hesitation. "Yup. That's why they call it Scooptown."

"Do you have any brothers and sisters?" That came from Gram Katie.

Charlie gave a little laugh. "Nine of 'em to be exact."

"How nice to have big family," said Gram.

"When you're tenth in line for the outhouse, it feels kinda crowded."

I was the only one who laughed, although Uncle Morris did manage to crack a slight smile. "I understand you plan to be an actor," he said.

At this point, Uncle Steve barged in. "What do *you* know about acting?" he asked in a challenging tone.

"Not much. Only that it pays good."

A few glances were exchanged over Charlie's poor grammar.

"Charlie's going to be a big star. Don't you think he looks a lot like John Garfield?"

"Does the world need another one?" Uncle Steve said.

I glared at him, infuriated by his rudeness.

Uncle Steve pressed on. "What if you can't make a living acting?"

"Then I'll go back to being a soda jerk."

Aunt Sophye, almost spitting out her wine, blurted out, "You were a soda jerk?"

"He probably means when he was in high school," Uncle Morris said. He was trying to make nice.

"We can always find Charlie a job at the paper box factory, Mama, if it comes to that," Uncle Morris went on.

I felt this was my moment: "Thanks, Uncle Morris, but Charlie and I have other plans."

All eyes were on me. "Charlie and I are engaged."

Dead silence. I looked around the table at each stony face.

Finally, Uncle Morris broke the silence and raised his glass, "Mazel Tov."

My father reached out and gently forced Uncle Morris to lower his glass. "We need to talk about this."

"There's nothing to talk about," I said. "I'm eighteen and I'll do what I want."

"I thought you wanted to finish drama school."

"I'm putting it on hold."

"On hold is the kiss of death," said my father.

"You're quitting?" Aunt Sophye asked, incredulous.

"See? What did I tell you? I just threw my money right down the drain!"

"We're taking turns, Daddy, that's all. First it's Charlie's turn and then it's my turn."

"You'll never get your turn," Aunt Sophye said. "Mark my words."

I was distraught. "I thought you'd all be happy for me."

With that I got up from the table and ran into the kitchen.

Aunt Sophye followed.

Charlie stood up to come after me.

Gram Katie stopped him. "Mr. Buchinsky, remain in seat if you please."

Out of politeness, Charlie sat back down.

In the kitchen, Sophye and I were nose-to-nose, both of us furious and yelling.

"Why did you just sit there?" I shouted at her. "Why didn't you say something? I expected you to be on my side."

"Are you crazy? How could you even *think* of bringing a man like that into this house?"

I knew they could hear every word from the dining room.

Aunt Sophye went on. "I'm outraged."

"What's wrong with him?"

"You have to ask?"

"Yes!"

"He's low class. He's too old for you. He's got no prospects. He's not even Jewish."

I was livid. "Anything else?"

"Yeah, he's ugly!"

"*I* think he's handsome."

Aunt Sophye's derisive laughter filled the room.

"You're not the one marrying him. I'm the one marrying him."

"What you do affects the whole family. What if we don't want to be related to the Buchinskys of Scooptown for the rest of our lives?"

In the dining room Gram Katie was visibly upset. She turned to her son. "Steve, make them stop."

"Mama --"

"Quick, go in kitchen!"

Reluctantly, Uncle Steve got up and pushed his way through the swinging door and into the war zone.

He said, "Look, Harriett, I know that this is none of my business -- "

"That's right."

"Nobody wants to see you make a mistake."

"Shut up!"

That pushed a button. "Don't tell me to shut up!" Uncle Steve said.

"Shut up!"

I hauled off and gave Uncle Steve a punch in the chest.

"You stupid fool." He grabbed my forearm and twisted it back just enough to hurt. I shrieked.

Charlie appeared in the doorway. Calmly, he walked over to Uncle Steve and put his hand firmly on his shoulder.

"I suggest you let go," Charlie said threateningly, but ever so softly.

Uncle Steve let go.

"C'mon," Charlie said to me.

Robot-like, I followed him out of the kitchen.

"Thank you for dinner, Mrs. Fenkel," Charlie said politely to Gram Katie, shaking her hand. "We're leaving now."

Outside on the street I had to scramble to keep up with Charlie. He was walking rapidly to the trolley stop. I was struggling with the tangle of my coat -- my sleeve was inside out. I broke into a run.

"I'm so sorry!" I said.

"They're right. I have nothing to offer you."

"You have *you* to offer me."

"I'm wasting my time at Bessie V. Hicks."

Fear gripped me. "So what does that mean? What about me?"

Charlie looked me straight in the eye and said, "I'm taking you to Scooptown to meet *my* family."

# Chapter 11
## Scooptown

December 28, 1947, Cambria County, Pennsylvania. There had been a blizzard. We headed by Greyhound bus towards Ehrenfeld through breath-taking mountain scenery. The chains clang-clanged as we wound our way along a two-lane, snow-covered road.

Inside the bus, Charlie and I were bundled up. I wore my brown sheared beaver coat. Charlie wore two sweaters, a scarf and a hand-knit wool hat made by his mother.

He filled me in on who was going to be there. "My sister Anita's the deaf one, so make sure she can see your mouth when you talk. My sister Julie's been teaching her to read lips. Catherine's the family beauty. The others are Roy, Walter, Joe, Dempsey, Elizabeth, and Mary. My mother's also Mary. You got that?"

"I'm so nervous."

The bus drove down the main street of the town and stopped in front of a small hotel. We got out. A pick-up truck was waiting for us at the curb. Behind the wheel was one of Charlie's brothers.

We walked over to the truck.

"Joe, this is Harriett. Harriett, this is Hollywood Joe. We call him that because when he was a kid he always wanted to be a movie star."

"Now it's nothin' but the coal mine. Hiya, Harriett. So you're the society girl Charlie's been raving about. Welcome to Scooptown."

"Hi, Hollywood Joe," I said.

On the road to the Buchinsky's house (which no longer exists) we passed quiet poverty -- small houses with small efforts to decorate for Christmas. There was snow on every tree branch.

"So how do you like our town?" Hollywood Joe asked me.

"It's beautiful."

"Until the snow melts."

"How far do you live from here?"

"It's up the road from Nanty Glo in Cambria County, just across the Little Conemaugh River from South Fork," Joe said whimsically.

I smiled, "That's poetry."

"That's malarkey," Charlie said. "All he's saying is it's not far."

We arrived at a small, two-story house on a hilltop overlooking the No. 8 coal mine. There was an outhouse in the middle of the back yard. The driveway was crowded with cars and pick-ups belonging to visiting relatives. Christmas lights were draped over a leafless bush outside the front door.

Charlie's mother was the first one outside. Putting a shawl over her head, she ran down the front steps, grinning at us, followed by Dempsey, Charlie's favorite brother, and then an excited Anita who opened her mouth for snowflakes that came floating down from trees.

"Ma, this is Harriett. Harriett, this is my mother, Mary Buchinsky."

His mother hugged me. "Welcome, Darling."

She winked at Charlie. "She's pretty."

There were more greetings, embraces, and hugs as the rest of the Buchinsky clan surrounded us. I had never felt this warmly welcomed anywhere. I was ashamed of the way my family had reacted to Charlie. This was a splendid contrast.

The Buchinsky's living room was modestly furnished. There was a coal-burning stove in the kitchen. Charlie's brothers and sisters, ranging in age from seventeen on up to thirty-seven, all bore an uncanny family resemblance. Here I'd been thinking that Charlie was the most unique-looking man on earth -- and now I was in a whole room full of Buchinskys who looked just like him.

Their sense of fun and looseness, their commitment to each other, and their obvious interest in bettering themselves really appealed to me. You could feel the love even when they chided one another, which was often.

I felt really at home.

## Chapter 12
## New York, New York

After that disastrous dinner at Gram Katie's, my father ordered me not to see Charlie again. As far as the family was concerned, our engagement simply didn't exist. They dismissed it; they dismissed Charlie. I was supposed to get back on track and move ahead with my life.

Of course, I had no intension of giving up Charlie, so we went underground -- literally. We'd ride the subway under the streets of Philadelphia for hours, just to have a warm place to be together and kiss. Sometimes we'd surface for dinner and opera at Victor's Italian Restaurant in South Philadelphia, which was usually my treat since Charlie still had no money. And of course, sometimes we'd go to Charlie's room and make love.

Neither of us returned to Bessie V. Hicks for the second year. Charlie moved to New York to try to make it in the theatre while I worked at my Aunt Sophye's dress shop to make money. The family couldn't bring themselves to forgive me for thrusting Charlie into their midst. They were polite to me. They were formal. But never again was I their *sheine meydele* -- their beautiful girl who could do no wrong.

I had disappointed them beyond repair. The only relative who believed that what I felt for Charlie was true love was Uncle Morris. He never faltered in his love and support.

Once Charlie was settled in New York, I announced that the engagement was still on, and that I'd be going to New York every weekend to visit him. I cushioned the shock somewhat by telling my father that I'd be staying with my friend Honey who'd also left Bessie Hicks and was now living in Manhattan. Of course, I didn't stay with Honey. I stayed with Charlie.

"I'm telling you, he'll never marry you. He's just using you," my father said.

"That's not true, Daddy. As soon as Charlie has $500 saved we are going to get married."

"I'll believe that when I see it!"

Every weekend after I got paid, I'd take the train to New York to visit Charlie in his tenement apartment (six flights up) on West 113th Street. I'd give him the money I'd earned at Aunt Sophye's so he could pay his rent, buy food and start our "get married" fund. Already, I saw my earnings as "our" money.

Charlie's roommate at the time was another struggling actor, Jack Klugman. They both worked part-time delivering mail. In their room, there was an old-fashioned radiator in front of the window which is where Jack used to hang his wet clothes. It drove Charlie, the neat freak, crazy. They really were the odd couple – but they got along.

Jack was dating his soon-to-be wife, actress Brett Somers (who later become well-known as a panelist on the TV show, *Match Game*). If Brett was in the room, Jack would put a sign on the door: "Am rehearsing." When it was our turn to "rehearse," we would (aside from the obvious) lie down on the bed and listen to radio music, especially the very young Rosemary Clooney. Charlie predicted she'd be a star someday.

One of the songs that Rosemary Clooney sang was called *Forever and Ever*. It became "our song." Later, when Charlie bought my $42 gold wedding band at Barr's Jewelry in Philadelphia, he had it engraved "*Forever and Ever, Love Charlie.*"

The first gift that Charlie ever gave me was a twelve dollar framed pen and ink drawing of a cat. I'd stopped to admire it in a shop window on Broadway in New York. I still have it. While our daughter, Suzanne, was growing up, it was on her bedroom wall.

For Charlie, his year in New York was a frustrating one. He tried to break into the theatre and did manage to get a few small parts in a couple of *off*-off Broadway shows, but in the end he had to give it up and deliver mail (a job he hated) full time in order to pay bills.

It was during one of my trips to New York to visit Charlie that I became aware that he had a flaw -- jealousy.

We were sitting in a coffee shop one day drinking coffee (I'd gotten used to it, just as Charlie said I would) and eating honey buns when a good-looking man passed by our booth. Without thinking, I glanced up at him. When I looked back at Charlie his expression had changed -- it was black.

"Why do you flirt?" he said.

This came out of left field.

"What?"

"You were flirting with him?"

"What are you talking about?"

"I saw you." Charlie's jaw was tight.

"I *looked* at him."

"Never mind."

There was an uncomfortable silence. Then Charlie broke it. "I was just kidding."

I didn't know if I believed him or not. It was the first time I'd questioned his word. I looked away. He put his hand under my chin, tipped my face up. "Okay?" he said, almost pleading.

I wanted to believe him. "Okay."

We went on with our conversation, but it was a red flag. Once I'd seen it, it stayed there flapping in the breeze.

"I don't think this New York theatre thing is going to work out," he was saying -- as if nothing had happened. "I've applied to the Pasadena Playhouse in California."

Once again, I was gripped with fear at the idea of losing him. "California!"

"Whoa! Not right away. Jack and I just got jobs in Atlantic City for the summer. After that, if I get into the Pasadena Playhouse, I'll go out there first and get established. Then I'll send for you."

I knew one thing for sure: That was *not* a good idea.

"No," I said. "I'm going with you."

Charlie grinned. "I can see that."

## Chapter 13
## On the Boardwalk of Atlantic City

During the summer of 1948, Charlie and Jack Klugman took jobs at a bingo place on the Atlantic City boardwalk. It was called Thrillo. The place had long benches and long tables. Some people played the ten Thrillo cards upside down to make it more fun.

The establishment was run by the father of Ed McMahon (Johnny Carson's future sidekick), also named Ed. Charlie, Ed McMahon (the son), Jack Klugman and Charlie's old pal from drama school, Joe Roman (also working there), took turns giving the patrons the balls to throw into the slots in front of them. They would call out "T" or "H" to the person at the microphone who would then repeat it over the loud speaker. Charlie's hours were from four o'clock in the afternoon until two in the morning.

I'd spent most of my teenage summers in Atlantic City, as had many of my Philadelphia friends, so I knew the place well. I quit my job at Aunt Sophye's and got a job in a handkerchief and linen shop on the boardwalk, working from six to ten every night. After work, I'd go back to my father's cousin's rooming house where I was staying, take a nap, then get up, get dressed and walk to Thrillo and wait for Charlie to get off work.

Because of Charlie's jealousy problem, I had to remember to keep my eyes lowered – at Thrillo and everywhere else – or

Charlie would accuse me of flirting. I didn't like it, but I was so in love with him that I put up with it.

When Charlie finished work at two in the morning, we'd grab a sandwich and then walk along the boardwalk, singing old songs and walking in time to the tune. We'd end the evening sitting on my father's cousin's porch swing and neck for a couple of hours before Charlie left for his place, and I would retire to my quarters on the back porch bedroom to sleep.

In early September of 1949, Thrillo burned down. By that time Charlie had saved only $200 – and now he was out of work. My father, realizing that we were serious about this marriage thing, had a reluctant change of heart: "Tell you what," he said to me. "When Charlie saves a total of $250 I'll match it."

It didn't take us long. I put my salary into the pot and when we reached $250 my father matched it, as promised, and gave me his permission to marry Charlie. Even though I was of age and could have eloped, his okay was crucial to me.

As far as the rest of the family was concerned, I was "marrying down" so they refused to come to the wedding. Aunt Sophye called me a tramp. On the day of the wedding, she and Gram Katie sat *shiva* (a period of grief or mourning in the Jewish tradition) for my marriage! All the mirrors in the house were covered over with white sheets and photographs of me were turned to the wall. Only Uncle Morris sent a card wishing us well. From Uncle Steve, only silence.

Experiencing the prejudices of my own family members regarding Charlie brought back all those painful memories of the religious prejudice I had suffered during grammar school, junior high school and high school. However, the fact that Charlie wasn't Jewish didn't faze me. He wasn't the least bit like those people who had shunned me in school. And now he wasn't the least bit like those people in my own family who shunned me now.

## Chapter 14
### I Thee Wed

I sat in my father's Nash in my wedding dress, an ice-blue satin number with matching hat and shoes. I was holding my wedding bouquet.

"Why get married in Atlantic City? Why not get married in Philadelphia?" my father asked me.

"Charlie hates Philadelphia."

"Charlie has weird ideas. And no work I might add."

"We're doing it the way we want."

"What kind of man lets a woman support him? What about your acting?"

"I told you, it's on hold."

He paused a moment. "Here's the turnoff. We'll stop at Roosevelt Cemetery and visit your mother's grave."

"Do we have to? Isn't the family sitting shiva depressing enough?"

"It's the last chance you'll have to visit her."

"I'm going to California, not Siberia."

When I glanced over, I was surprised to see that there were tears in Sam Tendler's eyes. I realized that, in his way, he loved me and would miss me. I leaned over and kissed his cheek. "Thank you for coming to my wedding, Daddy. It means a lot to me."

We drove into Roosevelt Cemetery, parked, and walked over to my mother's gravestone: *"Frances Tendler: 1904-1932."*

We stood and bowed our heads.

"I'm getting married today, Mama. I wish you could be here to see me." Then I turned to my father. "I don't even remember her. How come I can't feel anything?"

"You were too young. But you remember," he said pointing to his heart, "in here."

I broke off a flower from my wedding bouquet and placed it on my mother's grave. Then my father put his arm around me and we walked back to the car.

We pulled up in front of an old Victorian hotel. Charlie, in a navy suit, white shirt and blue tie was waiting for us at the curb.

Before Charlie reached the car, my father said, "Be glad you're not marrying a handsome man, otherwise you'd have to keep your eye on him. Why do you think your mother married me?"

"Oh, Daddy, stop. I think you're both handsome."

Charlie came over to the car, leaned into the open window.

"Hey, you look nice," he said to me. "Like something out of a fashion magazine."

In his hand, Charlie was holding the little box with my wedding ring in it.

"Look at the ring Charlie gave me, Daddy. It's inscribed *'Forever and Ever, Love, Charlie.'* Here, look."

"I'll take your word for it. So okay, where's the party?"

We were married at the City Hall in Atlantic City on September 30, 1949 by a Jewish judge as per my father's request. Before the ceremony, we picked up a witness, a lawyer, who kept fanning himself with his paperwork all the way through it.

Afterwards, we said our goodbyes on the boardwalk. I clung onto my father, crying, "What if I never see you again." I was getting a stomach ache.

"You're only going to California, not Siberia."

That evening Charlie and I went dancing at the Traymore Hotel where we had a near-miss jealousy incident. Fortunately, I had noticed on the way to our table that our waiter was good-looking. As he headed our way, I quickly looked down at my menu and kept my eyes down until Charlie had ordered and the waiter walked away. Satisfied that I wasn't "flirting," Charlie's mood stayed up and we danced the Anniversary Waltz. Charlie was a terrific dancer. When we lived in Hollywood later on we went out dancing at clubs such as Ciro's, Mocambo, the Cocoanut Grove and the Hollywood Palladium. It was great fun.

The next morning Charlie and I got on the bus for Los Angeles with all our worldly goods -- $250 in cash (left over after paying for the wedding and hotel), five suitcases (four of them mine) and a black umbrella. I couldn't have been happier.

# BRONSON FAMILY ALBUM
## PART 1

(Above) March 1928 - My mother, Frances Tendler, four years before her death from being thrown by her horse. (Below, left) August 1930: Me at 10 months with my mother. (Below, right) 1930: Me as baby with my father.

Above, Sam Temdler & Me.
Left, Framces Temdler & Me.

(Above) July 4th, 1930 – Me with my parents.
(Below, l to r) May 14, 1931 - My Aunt Sophye,
me, my mother and my grandmother, Gram Katie.

(Left) My mother in her favorite outfit – jodhpurs; (Above) 1931- Me with my father. (Below, left) August 1931 – Me at almost two; (Below, right) Me at four.

1947 – Cast of the "Junior Miss" production at Springfield Township High School. I had the lead role. (I'm the 2nd from the left, front row).

"CINCHONA FARM," Pennsylvania - 1940s

Digitech Photo

Charlie Buchinsky (top row, extreme left) in World War II where he served as a B-29 tail gunner. Meanwhile, I was finishing up grade school and high school, graduating in 1947. (Below, right) Me as a teenager.

Springfield High School

Charlie and I met in September of 1947 at the water fountain at The Bessie V. Hicks School of Stage, Screen and Radio in Philadelphia. Charlie said the word "C'mere" – and I *did* – and that word changed my life forever. Below, somebody wrote "Helen Hayes" in my yearbook because of my interest in the theatre.

HARRIET DORIS TENDLER
"Hats"

357 Haws Lane, Philadelphia 18, Pa.

Whether planning a super-colossal gym exhibition, expressing opinions about the inherent goodness of man in P. O. D. class, or being a mainstay of the dramatic club, Hats maintains her title of Springfield's champion live wire.

Dramatic Club 9, 10, 11, 12; Interclass Hockey 10; Interclass Basketball 10, 12; School Play 11, 12; Interclass Tennis 12.

Photo: Classic Studio

1947 – Charlie's first professional headshot, which he gave to me as a gift.

(Above) Atlantic City, New Jersey. I took this picture of Charlie in 1948, the year before we got married. He was working at a bingo hall called THRILLO. (Below) I do a bit of cheesecake myself in California in the 1950's

# WEDDING DAY SEPTEMBER 30, 1949
## Atlantic City, N.J.

Photos by Fred Hess & Son

Snapshot taken by my father on the boardwalk.

## California Here We Come!

Stop-over at an Oklahoma motel while I recovered from the flu. Then, it was back on the Greyhound bus to L.A.

## Chapter 15
## The Buchinsky Five-Year Plan
## for Success and Happiness

Like many who choose acting as a profession, Charlie and I had a Five-Year Plan for Charlie's success. If he didn't make it in Hollywood within five years, we were going to turn around and go home where, he said, "I'll be a beach bum."

The countdown began at 4 a.m. on October 5, 1949, when our Greyhound bus pulled into the bus station in downtown Los Angeles. We took the "red car" (a trolley that doesn't exist today) to Pasadena where Charlie was already enrolled in the Pasadena Playhouse.

I was glued to the window looking at the lush vistas -- the mountains, the palm trees, the flowers, the fancy cars, the mansions, the billboards. "I can't believe we're actually in California," I kept saying.

We rented a tiny two-room "porch" apartment at the back of a house on El Molino Avenue, furnished with a rattan couch and chair. Off the living room was a tiny bedroom with a double bed, dresser, bedside table and a straight chair. The kitchen consisted of a small refrigerator with a four-burner hot plate on top.

"Where's the kitchen sink?" I asked our new landlady.

"In the bathroom," she said.

"You mean there *is* no kitchen sink."

"So what do you think?" Charlie asked me.

"I love it."

"We'll take it. How much?"

"Sixty dollars a month. You're an actor?"

Charlie nodded.

"In advance."

Charlie handed over the cash, scooped me up in his arms and carried me over the threshold.

While Charlie went to classes at the Pasadena Playhouse, I went to work in a nearby department store called Mather's where I sold handbags for $27.00 a week. Charlie and I were a partnership. The money I earned was so that Charlie wouldn't have to think about anything except acting.

At the time it seemed natural for me to shelve my own ambitions for Charlie's; natural to jump up fourteen times a day to bring him coffee; natural to iron his shirts "no creases" the way he liked them. My reasoning was, *What's good for Charlie is good for me also.* In addition to my salary, he was getting $120 a month on the GI Bill.

So for our first years in California, we focused exclusively on Charlie's career, even deciding to put off having children until our mission of his making a living as an actor (so I could stop working) was accomplished. Charlie's career was "our project." We ate, slept and breathed Charlie's career. We had tunnel vision. I'm convinced, even today, that in order to make it in Hollywood -- and in a lot of other careers as well -- you *have* to have tunnel vision. We knew other actors who had day jobs, who had kids to support, and we could see how it held them back. I didn't want that for Charlie. I wanted him to have a clear shot at it with no distractions.

What made it easy was my conviction that Charlie would succeed. There was never a doubt in my mind. I'd already *visualized* his face up on the screen in my "mind's eye," and now it was just a matter of doing the necessary footwork to make that vision into a reality.

While it's true that I encouraged him, waited on him and helped support him financially, I didn't *make* him into Charles Bronson. He did that. He did it with an inner drive and a solid work ethic. He was the poster boy for what Woody Allen once said: "The secret of success is showing up." Charlie always showed up, on time, and well prepared. It was much appreciated in Hollywood and did wonders for his career. My main contribution was not getting pregnant and staying out of his way.

Aside from the fact that I found Charlie handsome and physically appealing, we had fun together. We enjoyed talking. He was not an intellectual but he was street smart and had common sense. I liked the way he sliced to the essence of things. I would sit on his lap with my head on his shoulder while he studied his scripts. I would give him his lines. He always expressed his love for me and I would respond in kind.

There was nothing phony or pretentious about Charlie. What you saw was what you got. He said what he meant and meant what he said. And we were on the same page as far as our values and goals were concerned.

His jealousy was another matter which I was eventually forced to deal with or it was going to ruin us.

No matter how successful he got as an actor, Charlie continued to maintain that he was in the acting profession for the money and not for the art. It was strictly business. It was not complicated.

After Charlie had been at the Pasadena Playhouse for a year, he came home one night with good news.

"They're putting me in a play."

"Oh, my God! What's it called?"

"*The Last Mile*. I play a convict named Killer Mears. They needed an ugly face."

"You're not ugly!"

"What do you know, farm girl?"
He grabbed me and kissed me.

When the play opened, Charlie and I arrived at the
Pasadena Playhouse early so we'd have a chance to look
around. I studied the publicity photos of Charlie in prison
garb in the glass showcases outside the theatre.

All I could think was: "I wish Daddy and my family were
here to see this."

After the show, I excitedly made my way back stage with
the crowd. I found Charlie standing with fellow actor, Steve,
and his pretty, red-headed fiancé, Kitty, both in their twenties.
Charlie introduced everybody.

"You were both great," I said to Charlie and Steve.

"And we're starving," Steve answered. "Let's go eat."

We found a coffee shop and piled into a booth, grabbing
four menus. In a booth across the aisle was another couple.
The man was facing me and I glanced at him, but then,
remembering, I quickly glanced away.

Too late. Charlie saw me. He leaned closer, "Why did you
look at him?"

"I didn't."

"I saw you."

A waitress approached.

"Charlie, what are you having?" Steve asked.

"Soft-boiled eggs."

"Jeez, live a little." Steve turned back to the waitress.
"Gimme a burger, everything on it."

While the men were ordering, Kitty, concern on her face,
whispered, "What was *that* about?"

She had obviously overheard my little exchange with
Charlie.

"He does that."

"If he did that to me I'd deck him."

I gave Kitty a baffled look, but I knew exactly what she meant only I couldn't deal with it -- yet.

"I didn't mean that. I'm sorry." Kitty sat back.

"What are you having, Kitty?" Steve asked.

"BLT on whole wheat. Lots of mayo."

"Harriett?"

"Apple pie and coffee."

"Are you sure?" Charlie asked. "That's 400 calories right there."

"Just coffee," I said tiredly.

"Good girl," Charlie said.

I felt like doing just what Kitty had said – decking him.

Later that night when we got back to the El Molino apartment, Charlie started his exercise routine. He stood between two chairs and started with deep knee bends.

I did a couple of half-hearted sit-ups, but stopped. My heart wasn't in it.

"Did you do seventy-five? What about your squats?"

"I'm too tired. Aren't you tired? You opened in a show tonight."

"You're not self-disciplined. Maintaining a good body is important. If you want something, you have to work for it."

"I know that."

"Then do it. Don't make excuses."

I started exercising again, fighting it.

Charlie went back to his knee bends. "You don't know how lucky you are being married to me."

"Yes, I do."

"I don't think you do. Most men aren't built like me."

"It's not just your body that I'm attracted to. It's the whole package; it's your brain; it's how you move; it's your conversation."

"You wouldn't say that if I had a big belly."

"It's still not the main reason I love you."

"If you love me so much then why do you flirt?"

I let out a deep sigh and got up from the floor. "I don't want to discuss this."

I went into the bedroom and closed the door. As I was doing so I got a glimpse of Charlie as he shrugged and went back to exercising.

The next day at Mather's Department store I was behind the handbag counter when I saw Charlie outside. He tapped on the window to get my attention.

I went outside. He was leaning against a car. "You still in a bad mood?" he asked.

"Me?"

"This will cheer you up. I just got a part in the new Gary Cooper picture."

He was right. I snapped right out of it. "A movie! How did that happen?"

"They were scouting for a mean-looking s.o.b. to play a Polish sailor, so they came to the school and right away my teacher says, 'Charlie Buchinsky.'"

"I can't wait to call Daddy."

As soon as I got home from work, I rushed to the phone.

"It's called *You're in the Navy Now*. And, Daddy, Charlie's even got a couple of scenes with Gary Cooper himself," I gushed. "I told you he'd make it, didn't I?"

My father was his usual self: "Don't count your chickens before they're hatched, Harriett. It could just be a fluke."

## Chapter 16
## Locations Blues

"Tell me more about the Gary Cooper movie," I said to Charlie. "I want all the details. Every single one of them."

"I'll know more when I get to Norfolk."

"Norfolk?"

"Virginia. It's a location picture."

"You didn't tell me that."

"What difference does it make?"

"You'll be going away."

"Just for a couple of weeks."

"I'll be here alone."

"So?"

"We moved all the way to California's because that's where they make movies -- and now you're turning around and going *back* again? It doesn't make sense."

"What the hell's the matter with you?"

"I don't like being abandoned."

"Have you gone bananas? This is what we decided to do. It's part of my job."

"I hate that part."

When he saw my anxious face, he softened slightly.

"Let's go into Hollywood and see a movie."

That was always a good distraction. A movie.

When Charlie left for Norfolk, I kept working at my job at Mather's. Occasionally, Kitty would join me on my lunch break at a local coffee shop.

"Thanks for the company. I hate being alone."

"You better get used to it, kiddo," she said.

"Did I tell you Charlie called me from Norfolk? He got an agent. Meyer Mishkin took him on."

"Meyer Mishkin? All right! He's really gettin' up there."

"Meyer told him he's going to make it big."

"Then Meyer's gonna be a happy man because ten percent of big ain't bad."

"Charlie's brothers Dempsey and Joe are thinking about moving out here."

"Being related to big ain't bad either."

"Charlie told them he'd help them get settled. That's so nice of him, don't you think?"

"Listen, Hon, I'm not saying this to be mean. You know I love you, but do you ever talk about anything but Charlie?"

"Why?"

"The man's three thousand miles away but it's like there's three of us here at the table – you, me and Charlie."

"I'm sorry."

"Just an observation."

"Charlie's my whole life."

"You didn't have a life before?"

I looked at her, genuinely perplexed.

"Never mind," Kitty went on. "Let's enjoy lunch."

When Charlie returned from Norfolk, I met him at the airport. As he got off the plane, he was flanked by three young women. I greeted him with a kiss, and they scattered.

"Who are they?"

"Production crew. Hey, I got me another part."

I forgot about the women. I was now all smiles.

"Daddy can't say the Gary Cooper picture was just a fluke now."

## Chapter 17
## Red Flags and Green Eyed Monsters

Charlie was easy to live with and never boring. He was thoughtful, neat, punctual, considerate, complimentary and kind. He loved me and he appreciated me. He was the perfect man.

Except for that one little thing -- his jealousy.

His jealousy was starting to drive me crazy.

If we were out and there was a man within a hundred yards, he'd accuse me of flirting with him. He'd watch my eyes to see where they were looking, so that trick I learned of looking down was now permanent. I was going through my days with my eyes lowered, always looking at my feet. I was even afraid to talk to some of the men we knew, like Steve, someone we saw frequently since he was also at the Pasadena Playhouse.

At first I tried to explain Charlie's jealousy away by "understanding" it – that it was probably because he was insecure. But then I'd think, *dammit,* I'm insecure, too! I'm the one who lost my mother when I was so young, but I don't pull that jealousy stuff on him and make him miserable over something he had nothing to do with. I, at least, had the decency (I kept telling myself) to turn my fears in upon myself and get stomach aches instead.

Whatever the root cause of Charlie's jealousy, it was getting to the point where I didn't care about the *why* of it – I just wanted it to stop.

The "last straw" episode that finally put an end to this glitch in Charlie's otherwise good behavior happened one windy day when it was pouring rain.

I was walking up the hill on El Molino Avenue, carrying a basket of folded laundry from the Laundromat and struggling with our huge black umbrella, when our friend, Steve, drove by, saw me, stopped and backed up. He rolled down the window.

"You look like you could use a lift."

"Thanks, but I'm fine."

"It's pouring rain!"

"Charlie wouldn't like it."

"You gotta be kidding!" Steve said. "That's nuts. You do know that, don't you?"

He rolled the window back up and drove on up the hill.

When I got home, Charlie was sitting in his new green leather chair, a script open on his lap, his eyes closed, listening to Rosemary Clooney on the radio.

I dropped the laundry on the floor. *Thump!*

Charlie, startled, woke up. "Why'd you do that?"

"I'm mad," I said.

"At what?"

"At *you.*"

"What'd I do?"

"It's your stupid jealousy. It's raining and Steve just offered me a ride and I was afraid to take it because I knew you'd be jealous."

"I should think you'd be flattered by it. It means I love you," Charlie said.

"I am not flattered by it. I am inconvenienced by it. It's driving me up a wall. If you don't stop it, I'm leaving you." I meant it.

I went into the bedroom and slammed the door.

After that incident, I had no way of knowing what was going on inside Charlie's head, but from then on all outward signs of jealousy on his part stopped. It never reared its ugly head again. If he felt it, he didn't show it. I was relieved. I didn't want to leave him but I would have unless he changed that behavior. I think Charlie knew I meant what I'd said. He "got" it that this wasn't an idle threat, and because he didn't want the marriage to end, he reined himself in.

Six weeks later Charlie bought us our first car -- a pale green Pontiac. "Now you won't have to walk home in the rain with your laundry," was all he said. And that was the end of it.

Later on in our marriage it would strike me as ironic that Charlie was the one who was jealous, yet he was also the one who ended up being unfaithful. When I mentioned this to a therapist friend of mine, she said, "A good rule of thumb is that extreme jealousy hides an unfaithful heart. It's called *projection* which means accusing others of what you yourself are feeling."

Considering how things turned out, that rule of thumb made perfect sense.

## Chapter 18
## Hollywood and Bronson

The acting parts in movies began to happen. After *You're in the Navy Now* with Gary Cooper came *The People Against O'Hara* with Spencer Tracy; *The Mob* with Broderick Crawford; *Red Skies of Montana* with Richard Widmark; *My Six Convicts* with Gilbert Roland; and *House of Wax* with Vincent Price.

For *House of Wax*, a wax replica was made of Charlie's head -- eyes, hair, everything was exactly like Charlie. After the movie was completed, Charlie brought the head home. "Let's put it in the front window to scare burglars away," he said.

I was terrified of the wax head. "Let's put it in the coat closet." It eventually ended up in a wax museum in Buena Park, California where there was a display of a body in an electric chair. The head on the body was Charlie's.

Here again, Charlie's work ethic had a lot to do with his growing success. The fact that he was always on time, knew his lines, was serious about things and never caused any trouble impressed some of the excellent directors he worked with and they brought him along with them on future movies. Co-workers, however, sometimes found his quiet style intimidating. He'd sit on the sidelines and watch, saying little.

He was talkative with friends, but socially he wasn't into chit-chat or long, drawn-out stories or conversations.

We moved out of the little back porch apartment on El Molino in Pasadena and into an apartment in Hollywood with a view of the Hollywood sign. I continued to work in various dress shops along Hollywood Boulevard, and we began to acquire *things*. I'd write home all about it. And I kept trying to impress my family with Charlie's successes. I'd send them "Charlie clippings" from the newspapers. *"Do you believe me about Charlie now?"* I'd write along the tops of the articles. Years later I learned that Gram Katie, Aunt Sophye and Uncle Steve all used to throw my letters in the trash unopened. Only Uncle Morris opened and kept his.

Up until now, Charlie had been using his real name, Buchinsky. Charlie's new agent, Meyer Mishkin, a short dapper man with glasses, dropped in one day to talk to Charlie about changing it.

We sat in our new living room on our new couch. The new TV set was tuned in to the Army-McCarthy hearings. Senator McCarthy's angry face filled the screen.

I served coffee. "Sugar, Mr. Mishkin."

"Make me feel like a hundred, why don't you! Call me Meyer. No sugar, thanks."

He turned his attention to Charlie. "There's a part in the new Alan Ladd picture. You're perfect for it."

"You giving it to me or do I have to read for it?" Charlie asked him, flashing him a smirk.

"Will you listen to him? -- 'Do I have to read for it?' It's called *Drum Beat* and Warners wants to see you about co-starring. They love you over at Warners. You'll get separate on-screen billing, so if you want to change your name, now's the time to do it."

That got my attention. "What's this about changing our name?"

Charlie had obviously been thinking about this for a while, but he had never said anything to me. "I'm tired of being typecast as a Polish sailor."

Meyer leaned forward in his seat. "Charlie, *Polish* isn't the problem. The problem is this communism thing." He nodded towards McCarthy's face on the TV screen. "It's got everybody on edge and frankly Buchinsky sounds too Russian."

"It's Lithuanian," I said.

"Yeah, but who *knows* that?"

"Charlie thinks actors should stay out of politics."

By saying that, I'd just given Meyer his next argument. His shrewd little mind went to work: "My point exactly. With Buchinsky, you're political whether you like it or not. Change it to something ordinary and you'll be done with the politics of it once and for all."

"Change it to what?" Charlie asked.

"That's up to you," Meyer said. "But make it American and make it snappy."


An hour later, Charlie and I were in the front seat of the pale green Pontiac with Steve and Kitty (now married) in the back seat, cruising east on Hollywood Boulevard looking at street signs to give us ideas for Charlie's new name.

"Why not just shorten Buchinsky to Bush," Kitty said.

"Too short," Charlie said.

"Bushin?"

"Too soft. Rhymes with 'cushion,'" said Steve .

"How about Charles Bogart? Charles Cagney?" Kitty, laughing, was on a roll. "Charlie Widmark? Charlie Gable? Charlie G. Robinson?"

Groans all around. We passed a street sign, Ivar Street.

"Charles Ivar?" This from Steve .

"That sounds more Russian than Buchinsky," said Kitty.

We passed Cahuenga Boulevard.

"There you go. Charlie Cahuenga!"

"God, no! Then I'd be Harriett Cahuenga."

Kitty laughed. "I love it, Harriett. Here's your chance to finally get into show business as the new South American bombshell, Senorita Harrietta Cahuenga from Caracas! You could wear a long red form-fitting dress, a flower in your hair, a black lace fan, castanets. Arriba! Arriba!" Arms flying, Kitty imitated a flamenco dancer.

We were still laughing when we stopped at a red light and saw a sign for Bronson Avenue.

"That's it!" said Steve.

We all thought about it. Bronson? Hmm.

Nobody had any objections.

Steve summed things up: "It's simple. It's got the letter 'B.' It's not taken. It's nondescript and it won't type cast you. It's perfect."

We all looked at Charlie.

"It's okay," he said.

"You better grab it, Charlie, because if you don't, I will. 'Steve Bronson.' Has a ring to it."

"I'll take it! You can be Stevie Cahuenga."

## Chapter 19
## The Wives' Code of Secrecy

In 1955, after five years and right on schedule according to the Buchinsky Five-Year Plan for Success and Happiness, our daughter, Suzanne, was born. Since Charlie's name had been changed legally, she was Suzanne Frances (after my mother) Bronson right from the gate. We were thrilled to welcome our baby girl into the family.

Charlie was crazy about Suzanne and vice-versa. For him, being one of ten kids, a baby was nothing to be afraid of. He could change diapers with ease. When she got older she'd jump into his lap the moment he got home from work, even after a fourteen-hour day, and he'd read to her.

Our friends used to comment on how good Charlie was with children -- especially after our second child, Anthony (Tony), was born six years later in 1961. Charlie was, indeed, an incredible father.

It was harder for me. I worried about everything.

"Sometimes I think you like kids better than grown-ups," I said to him.

"They're more honest."

"Who's not being honest with you?" I asked.

"Most people," was his answer.

I suspected that the reason he liked children so much was because they didn't challenge him. They looked up to him.

They were not a threat in any way. When older kids -- like the teenage sons and daughters of friends and relatives, for example -- challenged him, that didn't sit well with Charlie and he would sometimes say things that put them down. Nor did he like it when I disagreed with him. He'd respond with, "You're stupid," which hurt. He'd remind me that he was eight years older and had more life experience, and he'd get me believing that I *was* stupid. Today, we'd probably consider this "verbal abuse," but at the time I bought into it. Years later I realized that what was "stupid" was that I believed his negative statements about me.

However, with the exception of a few glitches in Charlie's make-up (and the jealousy glitch had gone), we were mostly in sync.

As "Charles Bronson," Charlie's career exploded. It was more than either one of us had anticipated. The more successful Charlie got, the more he became wary of people's interest in him, suspicious of their intensions. He worried that people would try to "brown-nose" him. He started resenting inquiries about how he was, as though they were intrusions into his private world. Another glitch.

And the money just kept coming in. Working at Aunt Sophye's dress shop and at the handbag counter at Mather's Department store all seemed like a hundred years ago. Now I was buying dresses and handbags, not selling them. One day Charlie surprised me with a brand new car. It was a Comet with a big red bow around it. I was thrilled. I now had my very own new car instead of Charlie's hand-me-downs. Life was good.

Some of the meatier roles Charlie was getting now involved that thing I hated -- going on location. Each new location brought on a new upset. The Big Stars of these movies got to bring their wives and children along on location, all paid for by the studio. They got drivers and nannies and tutors and roomy places to stay. But Charlie still wasn't a Big Star so we didn't get those things, which often meant months away from each other. We had bills to pay, not to mention remodeling expenses on our new house. Usually, I'd manage to visit a location for a week or two in the middle to break up the long lonely stretches. But then I'd have to return home again, leaving him alone (I thought), but in actuality leaving him vulnerable to the temptations of other women -- and all because I was trying to be "the good wife." Since Charlie never complained, I figured he was pleased about how responsibly I was handling the situation.

Still, whenever a new location shoot came up, we'd go through the same old routine.

"Do you *have* to go?"

"Yes."

"I don't like it."

"It goes with the territory. It's not going to change. Stop fighting it."

Round and round we'd go.

To stop, as usual, he'd suggest a movie.

One night after we'd seen *The Captain's Paradise,* we talked about the movie over dinner at Dupars.

"How could Alec Grinness have two wives without their finding out about each other?" I said. "That just couldn't happen."

"Maybe he was a good liar."

"Nobody's that good a liar."

"Maybe some wives don't want to know the truth," he said.

"I would."

"Look, it's just a movie. Let's enjoy dinner."

As Charlie was packing to leave for Mexico to film the movie *The Magnificent Seven,* I sat down on the edge of the bed.

"Mexico seems so far away."

"Three weeks from tonight I'll be buying you dinner in Cuernavaca."

"Three weeks is forever."

Charlie's patience was strained. "Harriett, stop doing this every time I go away. Find something of your own to do. Get a *hobby!*"

I remember pausing, and then I said: *"You're* my hobby."

Three weeks later I was, indeed, having dinner with Charlie in Cuernavaca.

It was hot there. The movie was being shot in rugged terrain. During the days I sat on the sidelines with some of the other wives, wearing a huge sombrero to shield me from the sun.

Charlie was in Western gear. A pretty young make-up artist was blotting the sweat off his face. One of the wives sitting near me, Bridget, in her forties, made a remark as Charlie took off his shirt and stepped in front of the camera.

"Your husband added that little bit of business all on his own."

"What little bit of business?"

"That taking-off-his-shirt-and-baring-his-chest little bit of business."

"He's got a nice chest. He exercises."

"This your first location shoot?" Bridget asked.

"It is. Yours?"

"More like my twenty-first."

"Are you an actress?"

"Gave it up. These days my career is keeping an eye on my man. He's that good-looking cowboy over there."

She pointed proudly to an ordinary-looking middle-aged man with a pot belly. "You can see why I'm so nervous. I wouldn't dare *not* be here."

"Why do you stay with him if you can't trust him?"

"I trust him fine when I'm here. You wouldn't believe the hanky-panky that goes on. Sooner or later most men succumb."

"Charlie's not like that."

"Of course, there are exceptions."

"Aren't the guys afraid their wives will find out?"

"'*Hear no evil, see no evil, speak no evil.*' The Wives' Code of Secrecy. Nobody talks. The wife comes; the girlfriend leaves. The wife leaves, the girlfriend comes back. Like those little figures in the Swiss clocks. Are you an actress?"

"We're taking turns. First it's Charlie's turn, then my turn."

"I've heard that one before."

She must have seen me flinch because she added: "Of course, there are exceptions to that, too. You don't have kids, which is good. They hold you back."

"I have a little girl," I said. "She's home with Charlie's brother and sister-in-law."

Bridget laughed. "I'm really putting my foot in it today, aren't I?"

At that moment, I looked over at Charlie on the set. I mouthed the words "I love you." Charles mouthed, "I love you" in return. I smiled. Obviously, we didn't have the kinds of problems Bridget was describing. We were different.

One night at the hotel in Cuernavaca I was tidying up while Charlie was taking a shower. I picked up one of his jackets to hang it up. I saw a letter sticking out of the pocket. I opened it. There was a note and a photograph of Charlie with his arm around a young woman. The note said, *"You don't have to be afraid of me. I won't bite you, Love, Janice."*

Holding the letter, I waited until Charlie got out of the shower. When he opened the bathroom door, I held out the letter.

"Who is Janice?"

"Just some crazy girl."

"Why are you in a photo with her?"

"Lots of people ask me to pose with them. She sent it to me."

He tried to be reassuring. "Don't worry, Harriett. The only women who ever come on to me are tramps."

For some reason that made me free better.

"And the men here who fool around are either unhappily married or emotionally sick. I am neither."

That made me feel better still.

"Why didn't you throw the letter away?"

"I forgot."

"Then I'll do it for you."

I ripped up the letter and the photo and flushed them down the toilet.

## Chapter 20
## Famous Friends

Hand in hand with Charlie's fame came famous friends. Jack Klugman was now in California and moving right on up the success ladder along with Charlie. We became close to Carolyn Jones and husband Aaron Spelling; Barbara Eden and husband Mike Ansara; Betty and Chuck Connors; Marilyn and Gene Nelson; Lee Marvin (unattached at the time); and Steve and Neile McQueen.

Whenever Jack came over, he and Charlie would be up to all hours of the night arguing about why they chose acting. Jack always said he was an actor for the creativity and Charlie, as usual, kept insisting his only goal was to make money. And yet they both succeeded.

In the early 1950s, Charlie got roles in anthology shows on TV, such as *Playhouse 90*; *The Defenders*; *Twilight Zone* and *Four-Star Theatre*. He co-starred in a half-hour drama for G.E. Theatre which, I believe, was called *Memory in White* with Sammy Davis Jr., hosted by Ronald Reagan. Sammy Davis Jr. had campaigned vigorously to get an Emmy nomination for Best Actor in that show, but Charlie, without campaigning, was nominated for a Best-Supporting Actor role. Even though Sammy didn't get a nomination, he was a wonderful sport and sent Charlie a telegram congratulating him.

We went to the Emmys. Charlie didn't win. The Emmy for Best Supporting Actor in 1954 went to Roddy MacDowell -- but we had a great time nonetheless. And we became friends with Sammy, who later invited us to his wedding to Mai Britt, a gorgeous blonde. In those days a mixed marriage was a truly rare event, making the wedding reception most interesting – with Sammy's family at one long table and Mai's family at another.

During this particular time period, I was pregnant with Suzanne. Sammy Davis Jr. was doing a one-man show at the Huntington Theatre and he invited us to come and see him perform. We got the time wrong and showed up late. When we entered the theatre and tried to sneak inconspicuously into our front-row seats, Sammy spotted us and stopped the show:

"I saw your empty seats and thought maybe you'd gone into labor!" he said. Of course, everyone laughed, as did we.

Many years later, long after my divorce from Charlie, Sammy was starring in *"Stop the World, I Want to Get Off"* at the Schubert Theater in Los Angeles. I took my son Tony to see the show and we went backstage afterwards so Tony could meet Sammy. Tony was as star-struck as I'd been at that age, and Sammy could not have been more gracious.

We gave a lot of parties. When Charlie's mother or my father came to visit, we'd have a huge party for them. We also had event and holiday parties -- baby showers; an annual Christmas Eve party; a big New Year's Day family dinner. On Christmas *day* we'd always go to Charlie's brother Joe's house. I was close to his wife, Jennie. On New Year's Eve, we'd go to the home of our friends Yvette and Hal. And we were always adding new friends to the mix.

And there was constant socializing with the Buchinsky clan, many of whom had moved to California to be near Charlie or they'd come out to L.A. for visits -- Joe, Roy, Walter, Anita, Elizabeth, Mary, Catherine, Julie and Dempsey all visited or moved here.

Neile McQueen, Steve McQueen's wife, became a favorite of mine. I first met her in Mexico during *The Magnificent Seven* shoot. She was fun to be around. Rules did not apply to her. When we were in Mexico, the women were all told to wear skirts; Neile wore pants. We did a lot of shopping together for lamps, vases and knick knacks, and we laughed a lot as we struggled to get all our bought items -- in huge big paper bags -- on the plane.

Neile and Steve were great together. He always referred to her as "my old lady," his term of endearment. Years later in the mid-1980's when I had a radio show on KIEV, I interviewed Neile after her memoir called *My Husband, My Friend* was published – all about her marriage to Steve and, sadly, their 1970 divorce. I was moved by her book.

Although we didn't see much of each other after our mutual divorces, every once in a while I would pick up my ringing phone and I would hear Neile's voice on the other end saying, *"And now there are six."* The next time it was: *"And now there are three..."* She was referring to the actors in *The Magnificent Seven* who had passed away. As of this writing, of the original seven, only one is still alive, Robert Vaughn. The six who are gone are Yul Brynner, Steve McQueen, Horst Buckholz, Brad Dexter, James Colburn -- and Charlie.

One time when my father came out to L.A. for a visit, Charlie and I gave a barbeque in his honor so we could introduce him to all our new friends. Hollywood Joe and his wife, Jennie; Dempsey and his wife, Anne; and Charlie's sister, Catherine and her doctor-husband, Joseph, were all there. (Catherine had followed her plan and found herself a doctor after all.)

"Hey, Joe, c'mere. I want you to meet a couple of your heroes," Charlie said.

Hollywood Joe followed Charlie across the back yard and over to Chuck Connors, who was talking with Steve and Neile McQueen. I was watching them.

I elbowed my father. "Daddy, do you see who Charlie and Joe are talking to over there?"

"They look kinda familiar. You're out of ketchup."

"It's Chuck Connors. You know, *The Rifleman.*"

"Everybody looks smaller when you see them in real life."

I went on, "And next to Chuck is Steve McQueen. Steve's been in lots of movies."

"Uh-huh."

"And that's Steve's wife, Neile. She's a good friend of mine. She's a dancer. She's been on Broadway."

"Neile is a man's name," my father said.

"It's her name, Daddy. And look, over there is Jack Klugman. Remember, he and Charlie were roommates in New York when Charlie was trying to do theatre?"

"That sure turned out to be a fiasco."

I pointed towards the pomegranate tree. "Daddy, look, do you see who that is under the tree? Lee Marvin. And the woman in the red blouse is Barbara Eden. You've seen them both on television."

"I hardly watch television."

I was irritated. "You *should!*" I took a breath. "Well, Daddy, do you think Charlie's good enough for me now?"

"Charlie's done very well for himself, I'll grant you that. Is there ketchup in the kitchen?"

I couldn't let it go. "Where do you want us to take you tomorrow? Disneyland? Knotts Berry Farm? Universal Studios? Farmer's Market? Anyplace you want to go. Just tell me."

"I thought this was supposed to be my vacation."

"I just want you to have a good time."

"I'm having a good time. Tell me where there's more ketchup and I'm a happy man."

Later I glanced over and saw Charlie brooding under the pomegranate tree. He was by himself, whittling on a piece of wood. I saw Lee Marvin go over to him.

"Downcast again, Charlie?"

"Yup."

"Sometimes I think you're too goddamn deep. Why don't you just take that coal miner's lamp off your head and lighten up. What's your problem?"

"I'm still making only $75,000 a year."

Lee Marvin grinned. "That's a problem?"

Charlie didn't answer him.

"Don't get greedy, Charlie."

"Why the hell not?"

"A guy can get caught up in it."

"Damned right!"


There were more and more movies, and more and more locations: *Miss Sadie Thompson* with Rita Hayworth; *Apache* with Burt Lancaster; *Kid Galahad* with Elvis Presley.

Meanwhile, Grace Kelly of Philadelphia married Prince Rainier III of Monaco. Another native of Philadelphia makes good. I was glued to the TV set.

## Chapter 21
### Mrs. Famous

Starting in 1958, Charlie starred in a TV series on ABC called *Man with a Camera*. He played Mike Kovac, a character based on a famous New York City crime photographer, Weege.

The show was a success and ran for three years, so for three years we had an almost normal home life – if you can call Charlie's thirteen and fourteen-hour days "normal." Still, it was better than when he was on location. He was home for dinner every night. I liked that.

For Charlie, the hardest part of the job was getting up in the morning. He hated getting up. He was a night person and loved to stay up until 4 a.m. reading, so when the alarm would go off at 6 a.m. it was a struggle getting him up. Sometimes he'd fall back to sleep on the bathroom floor. But somehow he always managed to drag himself out of the house and make it to work on time.

The show's sponsor was General Electric flash bulbs, so of course we had lots of flash bulbs for my Brownie camera. Charlie hated cameras, so I was the one who took pictures. There were other GE gifts, such as a TV and a stereo. We were accumulating more and more "stuff."

Charlie's salary skyrocketed. For all his worry about where his next meal was coming from, he worked constantly. Nor could he complain any longer about making "only $75,000 a year." When he went with the Kohner Agency, he was earning $500,000 a picture. Paul Kohner talked Charlie into hiring a publicist and promised him that by doing so, he would be paid a million dollars and 20% of the gross off the top of his next movie. Charlie responded by telling him that *if* that happened, he'd buy Kohner a Rolls Royce. It *did* happen -- and Kohner got his Rolls Royce.

Many of our friends were also doing TV series -- Steve McQueen was starring in *Wanted: Dead or Alive*; Chuck Connors was starring in *The Rifleman*; Barbara Eden was starring in *How to Marry a Millionaire*; and Michael Ansara (Barbara's husband) was starring in *Broken Arrow*. Actress Carolyn Jones was making a name for herself as a movie actress and her then-husband, Aaron Spelling, was a story editor on an anthology series. Richard Donner was a commercial director and directed the General Electric commercials on Charlie's *Man with a Camera* series. In the early 1960's, Charlie co-starred in Richard Donner's first directorial movie *X-15* which was shot at Edwards Air Force Base in Southern California.

There were more huge barbecues on Sundays with our friends (including a few from the neighborhood who were not in the entertainment business) and members of Charlie's family. Sometimes it's hard for people to understand, just by looking at Charlie, how much fun he was. He enjoyed himself. He enjoyed the people in his life. And he enjoyed getting rich and famous. In fact, we both enjoyed that.

He started painting again, which also gave him pleasure and satisfaction. He even had his own little art gallery in Beverly Hills where people could buy his work. But he hated parting with his paintings and at one point he went around and bought them all back!

In 1960, when Suzanne was five, Charlie was sent on a cross-country publicity tour for *Man with a Camera.* I got to accompany him -- to Chicago, Cleveland, Pittsburgh, Miami, New York and *Philadelphia.* We hired someone to come in to take care of Suzanne so I could go. I had just learned that I was pregnant again.

In Philadelphia, Charlie and I pulled up to our hotel in a cab. My father and his wife, Ann, the big blond, were with us.

There was a crowd of fans in front of the hotel, some carrying banners: "WE LOVE CHARLIE."

"Look, Ann! They're here just to see your son-in-law. Aren't you impressed?"

"Very," she said.

"Watch your purses when we get out, girls," my father said.

The doorman opened the car door. The four of us got out and walked towards the hotel. The fans behind the roped-off area began to chant: "Charles! Charles!"

Charlie looked uncomfortable. I was hanging onto his arm, but managed to wave.

"This is embarrassing," Charlie said.

"I think it's exciting." I was in my glory. I knew Gram Katie was in a hospital, seriously ill, but I thought that if only Aunt Sophye and Uncle Steve could be here to see all this, my rapture would have been complete.

A young male fan suddenly broke away from the crowd and appeared at Charlie's side.

"My girlfriend wants your autograph but she's afraid to ask."

"She should be," Charlie joked, and gave him an autograph.

I smiled with pride. Charlie may have hated the fuss, but he considered signing autographs part of his job and took it in stride.

Later that night Charlie, holding his photo-journalist's camera prop from the *Man With a Camera* show, spoke at the lavish Mastbaum Theatre and movie palace in downtown Philadelphia, the place I'd gone to so many times as a young girl to see Frank Sinatra and some of my other heroes. Now Charlie was on that stage. Uncle Morris was in the audience. I mouthed the words: "Aunt Sophye? Uncle Steve?" I was still holding out hope.

Uncle Morris shook his head: They're not coming. I turned away before he could see the tears in my eyes.

The next day I went to visit Gram Katie in the hospital where she lay dying. She was unconscious, tubes coming out of every orifice. I held her hand and talked to her non-stop. It was the first time I'd spoken to her in years.

"Gram, can you hear me?"

There was no sound. Only machine noises.

"Gram, please wake up. Are you still mad at me for marrying Charlie? Because it worked out okay. We've got a little girl, Suzanne. She's five. She's a great kid. She's your great granddaughter, think of that. I wish you could meet her. I think you'd love her a lot. And guess what, I'm having another baby."

There was still no response. I went on.

"You won't believe how well Charlie's acting is going. He's been in lots of movies with all kinds of famous stars. Are you listening, Gram?"

I heard a sound behind me and turned to see Uncle Morris standing in the doorway. He had been there a while.

"It's useless, Harriett. She's been in coma land for weeks."

"Uncle Morris!" I stood to embrace him.

"Hello there, Mrs. Famous."

"Are Aunt Sophye and Uncle Steve with you?"

Uncle Morris shook his head. I sat down, and took Gram Katie's hand again. Uncle Morris pulled up a chair next to me, and put his arm around my shoulder.

"How much more famous does Charlie have to get before the family will forgive me for marrying him?"

It wasn't a question Uncle Morris could answer, and he didn't even try.

I turned back to Gram Katie. "I forgive you, Gram, I really do. I know you love me. I know I'm still your darling *sheine meydele.*"

Six days after we got back to Los Angeles, Gram Katie died.

In 1961, Tony was born. While I was in labor, Charlie and I were still trying to decide on a name if we had a boy. We'd already decided on the name Julienne if it was a girl.

"What about Mike for a boy?" I said.

"If you go to a park and call out 'Mike!' half the kids there will come running."

"What about Mark?"

"Same thing for Mark."

My father's wife, Ann, suggested the name "Norman," which was her deceased son's name. In the Jewish faith, you usually name a child after someone in the family who has died – or at least a name similar to that name.

I said to Charlie, "I know -- let's name him Anthony after your brother who died? But only if we can call him Tony."

Charlie agreed.

Ten minutes later, Tony was born.

# BRONSON FAMILY ALBUM
## PART 2

### ARRIVAL IN CALIFORNIA

(Left) Our back porch apartment. (Above) El Molino house -- today it's a treatment center.

(Above) As newlyweds, Pasadena, 1950.
(Below) Our first Car, a pale green Pontiac
(Me -- and Charlie's shadow).

Charlie on the beach in Santa Monica, 1950

(Left) Charlie's photo was placed in the *Players Directory* by his agent, Meyer Mishkin, 1950's. (Right) 1950's Christmas in L.A.

## Charlie Begins to Climb the Hollywood Ladder

As Charlie got bigger and better roles, we began to be able to afford a few luxuries, such as a trip to Las Vegas in 1950 (above), and (below) a house in Cheviot Hills.

## Local Boy Makes Good

December 1958: Charlie was already getting famous when we visited his family in Ehrenfeld, Pennsylvania. It was big local news. (l to r) Me, Charlie, Charlie's Mother, Mary Buchinsky, and Charlie's brothers, Dempsey Buchinsky and Walter Buchinsky.

Photo: Delmar Watson Los Angeles Historical Archives

(Above) 1960 – Black and White Ball given by ABC for all their new TV Shows, including *Man with a Camera*. (Below) Nightspots – Mocambo & Ciro's

Photos Below: Los Angeles Times Magazine Feb 4, 1990

## General Electric Publicity for "Man with a Camera"

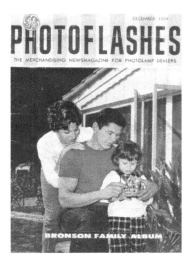

(Above) More Publicity Photos for "Man with a Camera."

Photos: ABC Photo: Bath & Wien

(Below) An "at home with" PR photo in our back yard.

Photo by Zinn Arthur & Bert Six

(Above, left to right) 1960: "Hollywood Joe" Buchinsky, Charlie, Dempsey Buchinsky and good friend, Red Ellis.
(Below) Charlie meets up with Dempsey during a personal appearance in Pittsburgh (where Dempsey lived) for some back stage kidding around with buttons that refer to Mike Kovac, the character Charlie played in "Man With a Camera."

8ᵗʰ Wedding Anniversary at Chasens Restaurant
in Beverly Hills. The event was sponsored by
the producers of "Man with a Camera."

(Above) Miami, 1960, Americana Hotel. We visit with my father and his wife, Ann, during our personal appearance tour for "Man with a Camera." (Below, left) My father and Ann. (Below, right) Our "last house" together, Motor Avenue in Cheviot Hills.

Publicity photos of the family
in 1959, here with Suzanne.

Photo by Zinn Arthur & Bert Six

Photo by Julian Wasser

This is one of my favorite pictures of our daughter, Suzanne, when she was about five. She is sitting in Charlie's favorite green leather chair.

Charlie with Tony – 1962
This is another of my favorite photos.

Photo: Delmar Watson Los Angeles Historical Archives

(Above) 1962 - The last photo of Charlie & Me together. It was taken at a restaurant in Germany while he was there on location for The Great Escape. (Below) Tony with Charlie on location in Turkey in the mid-1960's.

## Chapter 22
## Charlie's Great Escape

The location shoot in Germany for *The Great Escape*, to star Steve McQueen and James Gardner, was scheduled to last for three months. Once again, I was upset because Charlie was going to be away from me.

We were in the back yard. Suzanne was swinging in a new swing and Tony, now two, was on a new jungle gym. A housekeeper, dressed in white, was keeping a sharp eye on them both while I sat under a cheerful beach umbrella with Charlie, weeping.

"Three months is too long!"

"Harriett, please, not this again. This is my job. This is how I'm taking care of you and Suzanne and Tony."

Charlie looked over at the housekeeper and then at the maid who was at the back door talking to the guy from the diaper service.

"Do all these people have to be here all the time? It's like Grand Central Station."

"I want them here."

"I thought I married a farm girl."

"You married a farm girl who wanted to get *off* the farm." I got back to the subject of his location shoot.

"Is this movie so important?"

"*The Great Escape* might be the one to put me over the top and make me a major star."

He was right. He wasn't quite there yet. This movie could do the trick.

"I'm always afraid you won't come back."

"If you keep this up then one day maybe I won't."

I kept pressing my case. "Neile's going there to be with Steve for the whole time. Why can't I?"

"You *know* why, Harriett. We've been over this. Steve's the star. I'm not. If you and the kids came over to Munich for three months we'll have nothing to show for it when we get back. You want us to have the Cadillac, don't you?"

I nodded.

"And the new furniture?"

I nodded again.

"It's that or three months in Munich. Take your pick."

I picked the Cadillac and the new furniture -- and wondered if I was making the right choice. My friend, Kitty, didn't make it any easier. "You and the children should go with him," she said. "To heck with the Cadillac."

But I was convinced I was doing the right thing for us by staying behind so we'd have something to show for all Charlie's hard work when the shoot was over.

I flew over to Germany to visit Charlie six weeks later at what was supposed to be the half-way point.

Charlie picked me up at the airport. In the taxi on the way into Munich, I snuggled up close to him. "I can't believe I'm really in Europe." He gave me a little kiss. He seemed preoccupied.

After lunch in the hotel dining room, we went up to the room. I looked around. "Everything's so big here in Germany. The tubs are big. The forks are big. The pillows are big. I feel like Alice in Wonderland after she swollowed the shrinking medicine. Where are we going tonight?"

"To see the rushes. Did you bring a bikini?"

Strange question, I thought. "I don't own a bikini."

"Buy one. We're going swimming at David's and Jill's house on the lake."

"Who are David and Jill?"

"David McCallum and Jill Ireland. David's in the movie with me. Jill's his wife. They're English."

"Well *la-dee-da*."


I filled the bathtub to the top and got in. Charlie did his exercises between two chairs in the room. I could see him through the open bathroom door.

"This feels so good," I called out to him. "I have twenty-two hours of Lufthansa in every muscle."

Charlie looked in the mirror and touched his hair. "Son of a bitch barber. I told him not to cut my hair this way."

"I hate it when people don't do things the way you like because you always get so mad."

"They should do 'em right."


Charlie came into the bathroom with a lit candle and a vibrator. He was wearing only a towel tied around his waist. He turned off the overhead light.

"What are you doing?"

"Making for a little atmosphere."

He put the candle and the vibrator on the edge of the sink, dropped the towel and got into the bathtub with me.

Using a vibrator had never been part of our love-making routine, so it made me uncomfortable. "Where did that idea come from?"

"I just want to."

Suddenly, I felt wary. The whole idea turned me off.

"Well, I *don't* want to."

Abruptly, Charlie got out of the tub. He put his towel back on and left the bathroom.

When we were all dressed and ready to leave, Charlie said, "You're wearing that?"

"Why, what's wrong with it?"

"It's not very chic."

"You want me to change?"

"There's not enough time."

"What's wrong, Charlie, aren't you glad I'm here?"

"I thought I was trying to show you that in the bathtub."

"I felt funny about doing it there."

"You need a psychiatrist!"

"What's wrong?"

"Jesus, Harriett. We've got production problems, that's all. It has nothing to do with you."

"What kind of production problems?"

"It's Steve McQueen. He keeps asking for re-shoots. Now it looks like we're going to be here longer."

My heart sank. "How much longer?"

"Two months."

"No!"

"That's the way it is. Let's go. We're late."

In the screening room David McCallum, in his thirties, and his wife Jill Ireland, in her twenties, both blond and beautiful, were waiting for us. When we walked in Jill waved to us from down front. They were sitting with Neile and Steve McQueen.

"David, dear, Charlie's here," I heard her say in her very upper crust British accent.

We took seats behind them. Jill reached out her hand to me. "Harriett, I'm Jill, David's wife. David, stand up dear and meet Charlie's lovely Harriett."

David shook my hand. "I'm delighted to meet you."

Charlie turned to Jill. "You look lovely tonight. David, I think I'm going to steal your wife."

They both chuckled.

Neile McQueen sprang out of her seat and hugged me. "Thank God you're here!  Now I'll have somebody to see

Dachau with. These actors all think they're just too *sensitive* to go near it."

Steve McQueen turned in his seat. "Welcome to Kraut Town."

From the start, I was intimidated by Jill's beauty and self-assured manner. She struck me as *"veddy"* upper crust and worldly. She made me uncomfortable. I kept my feelings to myself because I saw how much Charlie valued their friendship (not knowing why at the time), but instinctively I felt out of place around them.

When the house lights went down, I took Charlie's arm and whispered, "They're nice."

"They've been good to me. David is like God."

"Like God?" Never had I heard Charlie sound so enthusiastic about anybody, let alone refer to someone as "like God." I wondered what it was all about.

A night scene from *The Great Escape* came onto the screen. Charlie could be seen crawling in a tunnel outside the barracks (filmed on a studio lot in Munich), stripped down to his undershirt, muscles showing, covered with dirt and sweat.

"That's *you!*" I said.

"Back on my belly in a tunnel just like I never left Scooptown. Only now they're paying me more for it."

The next day, Sunday, Jill and David invited the McQueens and us to their lakeside chalet in the Bavarian countryside.

Steve was at the wheel of the rental car. "It's probably Hitler's old place," he cracked. Neile was in the passenger seat. Charlie and I were in back. We sang *Red River Valley* and *The Girl That I Marry* as we sailed down the Autobahn. When we exited onto a side road, we passed a quaint country inn -- thatched roof, rambling roses, gurgling brook.

"What an adorable place," I said.

"Local shack-up joint," said Steve. "Known to be frequented by certain members of the cast and crew of *The Great Escape* and their frauleins, right Charlie?"

"That's what I hear," said Charlie.

As we pulled into the driveway of David's and Jill's chalet, Jill, looking particularly long-legged in her bikini, strode over to greet us. She ushered us out onto the patio overlooking a lake. She went inside the house and reappeared with a tray of cold drinks that sparkled in the sunlight. "What an amazing day!" she said.

She sat down next to Charlie and me. I tensed up. "Harriett, dear, I'm thinking of going to Paris for a few days. Would you like to come with me?"

"I'd love to, but I came all this way to see Charlie." I glanced over at Charlie. "I don't think he'd be very happy if I went running off to Paris."

I looked at him again for confirmation.

"I think you should do whatever you want to do," Charlie said.

"What a good husband you are," Jill said.

"I want to stay here with you," I said.

"And what a good wife you are. A great pity for me, though. Now I'll need to find myself another traveling companion."

She stood up: "Neile, how would you like to go to Paris for a few days?"

Later, Neile and I had a chance to sit on the terrace and talk in front of what looked like a movie backdrop -- a spectacular view of the lake and lush mountains.

"I hate your husband's perfectionism," I said. "Now it looks like Charlie's not going to be coming home for another three and a half months,"

"Stay here with him."

"I can't."

"Figure out a way."

"You sound like Kitty. I'm just trying to be practical."

"Charlie's lonely."

"He's not complaining to me," I said. "He seems to have made friends."

"That he has."

What I didn't understand was that Neile was trying to tell me something. She was trying to warn me. Apparently everyone knew about Charlie and Jill except me.

Steve came over and interrupted us. Only much later did I figure out that he was probably worried about what Neile was telling me.

"Hey, Harriett, what's my old lady bending your ear about now?"

Neile thought fast. "She's mad at you for all the re-shoots because it's keeping Charlie here longer."

Steve put his arms over his head in mock self-protection. "Yeah, yeah, I know. Everybody hates my guts right now, but you'll all kiss my ass when you see I'm right. You have to understand, Harriett, it's my face up there on the screen and if it doesn't look good, then the movie goes down the toilet and I don't work again."

Charlie wandered over in time to catch the last part of Steve's comment.

"You know what your problem is, Steve? Your problem is you spend too goddam much time getting into the part."

"Yeah, how do you do it, Charlie?"

"I show up. I say my lines. I go home. That's it."

"Maybe that's why I'm the star of this thing and you're not."

Everyone burst out laughing, including Charlie.

Jill came over and gave Steve's arm a playful jab. "Touché."

Later, in our hotel room, Charlie and I argued about the production delays.

"How can Steve get away with holding up production like this?"

"I don't know, but he's doing it."

"If I don't see you for another three and a half months I'll die."

"You won't die."

"Neile says I should stay."

"Is Neile paying for it?"

"Do *you* want me to stay?"

"That's up to you."

"I won't stay unless you want me to."

"You can't have it both ways, Harriett."

He grabbed his huge towel off the bed and walked into the bathroom.

I returned to America the next day.

Many years later, I learned that Jill Ireland and Neile McQueen did, indeed, take a trip to Paris together -- *after* I'd left Germany. I also learned that Steve had advised Neile that if Charlie were suddenly to show up in Paris, Neile was to return to Germany immediately. This information validated what I'd always suspected – that Charlie and Jill had started their affair in Germany and that everybody else did, indeed, know about it – except, of course, *me*.

## Chapter 23
## The Good Neighbor

I didn't realize it yet, but my world was about to fall apart.

*The Great Escape* was finally a wrap and Charlie came home. I saw the airline limo pull up to the curb. Charlie got out and the driver unloaded his bags to the sidewalk. Charlie waved to figures inside the limo as the children ran to greet him. The limo pulled away.

"Daddy!" Suzanne made a beeline for Charlie. Tony followed, "Daddy!"

The children threw themselves at Charlie. I came down the front walk and hugged him, one eye on the disappearing limo. "Who's that in the limo?"

"David and Jill."

"They're here?"

"David's doing a movie in Utah."

"Why didn't you ask them in?"

"They're tired." He turned his attention to the children. "Here, help Daddy with his bags."

The children struggled happily with the smaller bags. Charlie picked up the largest bag with one hand and put his other arm around me and we walked inside,

David had gotten a role in *The Greatest Story Ever Told,* which was soon to start filming in Utah. Jill hadn't been to Los Angeles before, so Charlie took it upon himself to find them a rental house and show them around. After only a few days, David had to leave for Utah on location. This time he left Jill behind.

Charlie, suddenly the Good Neighbor, spent his free days and evenings "helping Jill get settled in the new house" and "showing her where things are in Los Angeles."

"It's the least I can do to repay them for their months of hospitality to me in Germany," he said.

When I offered to take Jill around town myself, Charlie said no. "I'm the one they befriended, not you. I should be the one to do it."

Even then I wasn't suspicious. Jill was, after all, married.

"Charlie's being such a dear to drive me all around," Jill would tell me whenever we'd meet. She seemed so nice, so grateful. I even fancied Jill as my friend.

One day when she dropped by to pick up a Los Angeles map that Charlie had bought her, I decided to confide in her.

"I'm worried about Charlie," I told her. "Something's bothering him. He's restless all the time. He keeps running out of the house. Does he say anything to you?"

"I know he's upset about MCA folding and losing his agent."

"It's more than that," I answered. "He's moody. I know him. He's different. There's something wrong."

Jill looked me straight in the eye and, with great sincerity, said, "Maybe he's seeing another woman."

"Another woman!" I was incredulous. "That's just not possible. How could he be seeing another woman? He just got back from Germany."

Jill shrugged. "It was just a thought."

I decided to check it out with Charlie one evening while we were in the den. "I have to ask you something. Is there or was there another woman in your life during our marriage?"

"You're nuts." he said.

"Is there?"

"Of course not."

"*Was* there? In Germany?"

"Don't be ridiculous. You have a problem."

"Then what is *your* problem? Why are you so moody?"

I was beginning to feel that this was like the movie, *Gaslight*. Maybe I was imagining things.

"I don't know where my next job is coming from." He was back to that again. "I need to find a new agent. It's bothering me."

"Do you swear there's no other woman?" I wouldn't let it go. I went to the book shelf and pulled out the Bible. "Swear on the Bible there's no other woman. If there is and you lie about it your mother will die."

At that, Charlie headed for the door. "I don't believe this!"

"You didn't swear on the Bible!"

"You know what? You don't love me. You want to possess me."

"Swear on it!"

Charlie took me by the shoulders and shoved me against the door. Just as suddenly he let go, opened the door and walked out saying, "I don't want any part of this. I'm suffocating in here."

He slammed the door shut.

"Charlie!"

Moments later I heard his new Cadillac squealing out of the driveway.

Shaken, I walked out into the garage to confirm that he'd really left. He had. I went over to his work area where he painted and lifted the cloth over his latest painting in progress. It was of a man who looked like Charlie. The man was screaming. I quickly covered it up. I never mentioned to Charlie that I'd seen it.

I called my father immediately, "Daddy!"

"Hi, Harriett."

When I heard his voice on the phone, I started to cry. Since his marriage to Ann and the lifting of his depression, I could talk to him again.

"Daddy, something's wrong here."

I told him all about it -- about Charlie's strange behavior, the trip to Germany, all his dinners out "trying to get a new agent," and about Jill's statement that maybe Charlie was seeing another woman. "He *must* be having an affair."

"Don't be silly," my father said.

"But he wouldn't swear on the Bible."

"That proves nothing."

"You used to hate him. Now you're defending him?"

"So what are you going to do if you find out he's having an affair?"

"Leave him," I said firmly.

"You've got two children and a nice life out there in California. Don't push it."

"I have to know the truth."

"All right. Tell you what. Just to prove to you how wrong you are, hire a detective and have Charlie followed. I'll pay for it."

"Thank you, Daddy."

"Don't thank me. Sometimes it's better not to know things."

## Chapter 24
## The Beverly Hills Detective

Detective Kip Ameritti was discreetly staked out inside a non-descript car across the street from our house. When Charlie came out, got into his Cadillac and drove off, Kip followed.

Two hours later I got a phone call from Kip. "Nothing much to report, Harriett. He went to Santa Monica Pier, eyeballed some fish, got gas, and now he's on his way home."

"You have no idea how relieved I am."

"Anybody can have an innocent day."

The next day Charlie was babysitting the children so I could go Christmas shopping. He was playing with them on the jungle gym in the back when I drove into the driveway. I unloaded Christmas packages from the trunk and started carrying them into the house.

"It's about bloody time," Charlie said angrily. "I have an appointment."

"Again?"

"You want me to get an agent or not?"

He got into the car and drove off, leaving me standing there with the packages in my arms. Out of the corner of my eye I saw Kip Ameritti's car appear out of nowhere and take off after him.

Later while I was feeding the children, the phone rang.

"Harriett, it's Jill, dear. Is Charlie at home?"

"He's out."

"I see. Would you give him the message that I called? From Utah? I'm here visiting David."

"Okay."

"You'll remember to tell him?"

"I'll remember,"

"Thank you, dear, bye-bye now."

"What's he been doing?" I asked Kip when he called.

"He kept trying to get somebody on the phone from the gas station. Then he drove up to a house on Summit Drive, but no one was home so he left."

"That's David's and Jill's house."

"After that he went to see a re-release of *From Here to Eternity* in Westwood Village."

"He's already seen *From Here to Eternity.*"

"Well, he just saw it again."

By the time Charlie got home, I was in bed reading. I had told Jill I'd give Charlie her message, but by this time I was suspicious of her motives so I didn't tell him anything.

"Any calls?"

"No."

"No?"

"No."

"Oh," Charlie said. "I'm going downstairs to read. Are you sure there were no messages?"

"I'm sure."

A moment later, I heard the phone ring. Charlie picked up downstairs. The next thing I heard was Charlie's car pulling out of the driveway. I looked out the bedroom window in time to see Kip's car take off after him. Charlie was going like a bat out of hell.

Two hours later there was a call from Kip:

"I think we got 'em, Harriett. He picked up a tall blond from the airport and drove her to that house on Summit Drive.

"Jill," I said.

"Okay, so here's the plan," Kip went on. "I'm going to call the cops and tell them there's been a disturbance at Jill's address. My photographer and I will go up to the house, and when Jill opens the door for the cops, we'll be right behind them. You want to meet me there?"

"I'll be there."

When I arrived, Kip and the photographer were already on the scene. I pulled in next to Kip's car. The police car, just arriving, pulled in behind me.

Two cops got out. "This the house with the disturbance?"

"It will be soon," I said.

The four of us walked up to the house together. The cops looked into the front windows. The living room was dark. They went around to the back. Kip and I followed. They knocked. Jill answered. Inside, Charlie was sitting at the kitchen table with a cup of coffee.

We all pushed our way in. Charlie, looking stunned, jumped to his feet. "What the hell is this?"

"We have a report of a disturbance," said one of the cops.

"What are you doing here?" Charlie said to me.

"What are you doing here with *her*?" I said.

Jill whirled around to Charlie: "Would you please tell your busybody little wife to mind her own business."

"Who's this guy?" Now Charlie was glaring at Kip.

"The detective who's been following you," I said.

"You son-of-a-bitch!" Charlie took a swing at Kip and clipped his jaw. The fast-thinking photographer snapped a picture, then another.

Kip, clutching his jaw, ran outside, followed immediately by the photographer. They had what they'd come for.

"I don't like this one bit," Jill said.

"And I don't like your chasing after my husband one bit."

"Rubbish," she said.

I turned on Charlie. "No wonder you think David's like God. He's been sharing his wife with you."

One of the cops interrupted. "Look, folks, if this is just a domestic thing we'll be on our way."

"Yes, go!" Jill said

The cops left.

"Harriett, dear, why don't you go, too, and take Charlie with you. I don't want him here."

"No. You invited him here, so now you keep him. I'm handing him over to you on a silver platter."

"I'll decide who I want and who I don't want if you don't mind."

"Can we discuss this?" Charlie said.

I hissed at him. "There's nothing to discuss, you bastard!"

"Who's watching the children?"

"God!" Actually, Dempsey and Anne were watching them.

Charlie put out his hand, "Harriett -- "

"Go to hell!"

"You're acting like a crazy woman."

"You're *both* crazy," said Jill, and left the room.

I left and drove home,

When I woke up the next morning, Charlie was lying on the bed beside me, still dressed. He denied everything. "You're making a big mistake," he said. "There's nothing going on between Jill and me."

"No? So what were you doing there?"

"Having a cup of coffee. Jill's a friend. We talk about things. I didn't think you'd understand that."

"I don't understand that. Everything was fine until that big, horsy slut came along,"

"Harriett -- "

"What gives her the right to barge in and disrupt our lives?"

I pulled the covers over my head.

"Harriett, please -- "

"I want a divorce," I said from under the covers.

Charlie got up: "You will regret this for the rest of your life."

Charlie didn't want a divorce. He didn't even want to leave the house. For the next six months he slept on the couch in the den or in the guest room. He kept trying to reason with me, but it was non-negotiable.

I was overwhelmed with rage. Once when he tried to hug me, I scratched his face. I threw a knife at him. I threw rocks at his car. "You are nothing but garbage!"

Charlie couldn't understand the extent of my anger. How could I explain it? For eighteen years I'd loved him, trusted him, believed in his truthfulness and integrity, and now he'd betrayed me. The man living in the house with me wasn't even Charlie anymore. He was somebody else, and I didn't like him or want him. I felt overwhelmed and victimized by circumstances beyond my control, circumstances that the perpetrators would not even own up to. Charlie, Jill and David were doing whatever they pleased. They were wrecking my life and my children's lives without a care. It was like we didn't exist to them.

One morning I phoned David McCallum in Utah.

"David McCallum here."

"Are you aware your wife is seeing my husband?"

"Harriett?"

"Yes. Well *are* you?"

"They're friends."

"They're *sleeping* with each other!" I shouted at him.

"Harriett, don't bother me with these things," he said impatiently.

"Bother you? Did it ever occur to any of the three of you that maybe this is bothering *me*?"

"Come now."

"You don't care if your wife is sleeping with my husband?"

"Jill and I will sit down and discuss it in a civilized manner. I'm certainly not going to talk about it here on the telephone with you."

I couldn't help it. I laughed. "I forgot you British always *talk* about everything."

"You are being hysterical for no reason."

"My whole life is falling apart!"

"I don't know what to tell you."

"Listen, you self-centered, cavalier bastard. You tell your wife to get the hell away from my husband."

I slammed down the receiver.

## Chapter 25
## Christmas in Tinseltown

Christmas Eve 1963 came. Charlie and I were still living under the same roof and we were giving a party that had long been scheduled. The usual crowd was there. I'd decorated the rooms with candles, no electric lights. There was a fire in the fireplace, presents under the tree. Even the kitchen was lit only with candles.

Charlie was in the kitchen with me, putting hors d'oeuvres on trays. He was in a sour mood. "For someone who's Jewish, you really get into this Christmas thing with a vengeance, don't you?" he said. "I can't see a damn thing."

"I love Christmas," I said defensively.

"I love electricity." Charlie flipped on the overhead light.

Angrily, I turned it off.

"I don't know why you're even bothering to go through with this," he said. "We're not even speaking."

"I'm not disappointing my friends." I handed him a tray of hors d'oeuvres. "Here."

Later in the evening, Charlie walked out to the garage. He returned with an armload of beautifully wrapped Christmas gifts.

"These are for the kids from Jill," he told me.

"Jill bought gifts?"

Charlie nodded.

I took the gifts from his arms and headed straight for the fireplace where, one by one, I lobbed them into the flames.

The gifts made a luxurious glow. Our guests watched in stunned silence.

Without flinching, Charlie walked out of the living room and into his den.

"Hon, is there something I can do?" Barbara Eden asked me.

"What's going on?" said Neile McQueen.

Charlie's brother, Dempsey, stood up: "Anne and I are going to go on home, darlin'. Take care."

"I think we should probably all leave," said Kitty. She turned to me. "I'll call you tomorrow."

The guests embraced me and politely slipped out the door.

As soon as everyone was gone I went to the den.

"I want you out of here," I said.

"You got it!"


Later that night, Charlie was standing by his Cadillac with his shirts on hangers. "Aren't you going a bit far with this?"

"So who's going to iron your shirts now, Jill?"

"Jill doesn't iron shirts."

"Somehow I knew that."

"If I leave this house I'm finished, do you understand? I'm never coming back."

"Do you really expect me to go on here like this as though nothing has happened?"

"Nothing *did* happen."

On impulse, I pulled my wedding ring off my finger -- the ring that Charlie had had inscribed with *"Forever and Ever, Love, Charlie,"* and I threw it at him.

The ring ricocheted off his black leather jacket and rolled into the dirt.

Charlie leaned down, scooped up the ring and dropped it into his pocket.

"You can shove it up Jill's English ass!" I screamed at him and slammed back into the house.

When I got inside, Suzanne, now eight, and Tony, nearly three, were heading down the stairs. They'd been awakened by the shouting.

"Mom?" Suzanne said.

"Where's Daddy?" said Tony.

I hugged them both. "It's okay. We had a sort of fight. Come on, let's go back to bed." I took their hands and led them back upstairs.

"I want to see Santa with Daddy." Tony said.

"It'll take you," I said.

"I want Daddy to."

"Here's not *here*, stupid!" Suzanne pulled her hand away from me and ran upstairs.

## Chapter 26
## Sorry is More Than a Word

Once Charlie was gone from the house, I felt I had nothing. I was shocked to discover how emotionally dependent I had been on him. Not even Suzanne and Tony could fill the huge void. My self-esteem was at rock bottom. I had no career, no hobbies (other than Charlie, of course) to fall back on. I was a wreck, and overwhelmed with grief and anger that he'd betrayed my trust and had done "his thing" without any concern about me or our children.

Charlie, on the other hand, was resilient. He was coping just fine. His career was in full swing. He was getting more famous by the day. He kept insisting that he didn't want the divorce, but I felt I couldn't continue on with someone that I now saw in such an entirely different light.

We were at a stalemate.

Time dragged on.

It might have been more tolerable if Charlie had just admitted the affair, said he was sorry, reassured me that he loved me and didn't want to lose me, and promised me he'd never see Jill again -- *then*, maybe, we could have tried to repair the damage. But when he didn't do any of these things, it broke my heart and my spirit. Now that his emotional life was with Jill I wanted nothing more to do with him. Many marriages can survive an affair, but few can survive a *love* affair. What he had with Jill was apparently a love affair.

After that, everything became public. Getting separated from somebody famous isn't like getting separated from a bus driver. I couldn't even go to the supermarket for a quart of milk without seeing Charlie's face and Jill's face looking out at me from movie fan magazines: *Photoplay,* "David McCallum Loses His Wife to His Best Pal." *Inside Movie:* "David McCallum Asks, 'What Kind of Friend Steals Your Wife?; *Silver Screen:* "The Night Jill Ireland Forgot She Was Married." And *Movieland:* "Charles Bronson: The Man Waiting for the McCallums to Divorce."

I'd buy every single one of them.

"Why do you buy those things?" Kitty said to me one day when she was visiting and saw the pile of fan magazines on the coffee table. "They just make you cry."

"It's therapy for me, Kitty. When I read about Charlie and Jill in exotic locations, having tea in London, brioche in France, shrimp paella in Spain, and then I see Charlie putting Jill in his movies – and I compare all that to my own life, sitting zombie-like at my kitchen table, downing anti-depressants with a 7-Up chaser, and saving up Seconals 'just in case,' it's enlightening. It males me ask myself, where did I go wrong? What happened to *my* turn?"

"And the answer is?"

"I should never have ironed that first shirt!"

We both burst out laughing.

I hated Jill. I blamed her for everything. I was angrier at Jill than I was at Charlie. To me, Jill was toying with people's lives, with *my* life, as if I were little more than an expendable chess piece that she could push aside to clear the way towards her goal -- which was Charlie.

Some people we knew had a hard time understanding why I'd actually leave Charlie over his infidelity. I remember Steve McQueen coming to my house and saying, "You're crazy to leave Charlie." Members of Charlie's family approached me with the same message. I stuck to my guns. But living in this limbo state was reaching its saturation point.

One day, before the actual divorce, Charlie pulled up to the house in his new red Jeep Cherokee and knocked on the door,

I answered, still in my bathrobe.

"Don't you get dressed anymore?"

"What do you want?"

"I came to get my mail."

"Everybody knows you're living with Jill now so why don't you just have your mail forwarded over there?"

"Maybe I want to keep my options open."

I laughed, "How do you think Jill would like it if she knew you were standing here saying that to me?"

Charlie gave a non-committal shrug.

"I've learned more about you in the past couple of years than I want to know," I said.

"You put me on a pedestal and found out I have feet of clay."

"I don't want a man with feet of clay."

"Can't you let it go, Harriett?"

"Can't you say you're sorry?"

"I haven't done anything to be sorry about."

"You didn't keep up your end of our deal?"

"What deal?"

"That first it was going to be your turn and then it was going to be my turn. You never gave me my turn."

"How come you never *took* it?"

That caught me by surprise.

"I never knew I could."

## Chapter 27
## Loony Tunes

The divorce triggered a period in my life I referred to as my "walking nervous breakdown" -- dark depressons that snuck up on me without notice and would last for a week or so at a time. At one point I was convinced that Charlie and I were both dead -- that we'd died in a plane crash in Germany and were now invisible.

"You know that psychologist you told me about?" I asked Kitty one day. "Could I have his number?"

Fortunately, I didn't tell anybody else except this new therapist, Dr. Sanderson, about my crazy thoughts. I followed his instructions carefully. He said that as far as the rest of the world was concerned, I was to "pretend" to be alive, and not invisible, so they wouldn't come and take my kids away from me. I managed to keep up this "pretense" and kept the kids.

"Ever since Charlie left me I can't sleep," I complained to him one day.

"Left you? I thought you kicked him out on his ass."

"He abandoned me."

"Like your mother,"

"She didn't abandon me. She died,"

"Same difference. To a little kid it's just another kind of abandonment."

"She didn't mean to die."

"But she did it. And you're still mad at her for it."

"How can you be mad at a person for dying?" Then I added, "Can we *not* talk about this?"

"Sure we can *not* talk about this. What would you rather talk about?"

"I was hoping you'd send me to a hospital so I can get some sleep,"

"You'll be disappointed. They'll wake you up to make wallets."

"Then give me pills."

"I'm not a pill kind of doctor, Harriett, I'm a Ph.D. doctor. I'm a feelings guy. You have to *feel* what hurts before it will go away. The only way out is *through*."

"Catchy. But I don't want to feel what hurts. That hurts."

He said nothing.

I thought a moment. "Charlie hasn't even said he's sorry."

"That would make it all better?"

"At least I'd know I wasn't crazy."

"You're not crazy."

"How do you know that?"

"Because the hairs on the back of my neck don't stand up when I talk to you. That's how you know somebody's crazy."

I laughed. "You went through graduate school to learn that?"

"You actually laughed,"

"I feel better now," I said.

## Chapter 28
## The Devil Made Me Do It

It wasn't just therapy that cured me of my "walking nervous breakdown" after the divorce, it was Jill Ireland herself who helped me snap out of it.

Charlie and Jill were back in town. Jill got a part in a TV series called *Shane* with David Carradine, and Charlie bought an expensive one-story ranch house off Benedict Canyon -- only a stone's throw from Jill's -- which he was decorating in a very masculine style with black leather upholstery, new red carpeting throughout and wood paneling.

Jill decided to send Charlie over to inform me that she was not his *first* infidelity. She wanted him to make it clear to me that over the years he'd had a string of affairs.

Charlie stood in front of me and named names. Some were women I knew; others were even friends of mine.

Even though I was shocked and more than a little suspicious of Jill's motives in sending Charlie on this mission, and believed it to be self-serving, I was grateful for it. Now I could no longer delude myself that Jill was just a fluke and "if only" I'd done or said x, *y* or z, then it wouldn't have happened. I realized that if it hadn't been Jill it would have been somebody else. It was only a matter of time. This realization helped me let go of Charlie.

But I hadn't quite finished with him *yet*.

One warm summer night I got a bright idea. I think the devil made me think of it. In the divorce agreement, I'd been awarded the bulk of Charlie's paintings. Not paintings he owned; paintings he'd painted. In court they'd treated his paintings like furniture and since "the wife" got "the house and all the furniture," I got the paintings. Charlie was furious about it. *He* had painted them, he kept saying. They were *his* creations, not mine. Actually, I had no argument with that. I agreed with him. I didn't think that it was fair that they'd been handed over to me. But I stubbornly hung onto them. They were all I had left of him and it was hard to let them go.

But as time went on, I felt increasingly guilty about it. So on this night I thought, "I'll be nice and do the right thing and return them."

Throwing on a pair of jeans and a white sweater, I gathered up Charlie's paintings and put them in the car. The only ones I held back were those that were gifts to me, like the nude Charlie did of me when I was pregnant with Tony, and those that were of the children.

It was about eight fifteen and just starting to get dark when I arrived at the top of Benedict Canyon. I parked on the street. I'd already turned off my car lights when I noticed that the house was dark. I hadn't called. Obviously, Charlie wasn't home. I was about to leave when Charlie drove up the hill, pulled into the driveway and into the garage. Jill was in the car with him. They didn't notice my car. They got out and walked into the house. I waited a few minutes and then I went up to the front door with some of the paintings and rang the bell.

Charlie answered the door.

"Here," I said. "I thought I'd bring you back some of your paintings."

Jill was standing in the foyer behind Charlie. She was wearing jeans and a light summer top and her long, blond hair hung straight and loose over her shoulders.

"Hello, Jill," I said.

Without even a blink she said, "Shut up!"

I couldn't believe what I'd just heard. "Don't you tell me to shut up."

"Shut up, *cunt!*" Jill said in her clipped English accent.

I'd never heard anyone actually say that word aloud before. "Isn't that what I should be calling you."

Suddenly, Jill lunged at me. I tried to step back into the living room but wasn't fast enough. She knocked me to the floor and sat on me.

I struggled to get up but couldn't. Jill was a big, strong woman. At only 5'3" I was no match for her. I couldn't budge. I grabbed her long hair and started pulling it -- hard enough to distract her so I could wriggle out from under her. I broke free and jumped to my feet.

I was standing next to one of Charlie's black leather love seats when Jill lunged at me again. This time she pushed me over the back of the love seat. I rolled off onto the floor, and there she was again, sitting on top of me. Again, I pulled at her hair. She grabbed mine and gave it a yank.

I screamed, "Charlie! Get her off of me!"

Charlie made a weak attempt to pull Jill away, but she broke free and went for me again. This time I felt her fingernails on my face. My glasses went flying. Now there was blood on Charlie's new red carpet and on the front of my white sweater.

"Charlie, she's hurting me!"

I couldn't understand why he was allowing this to go on. I managed to twist my head in his direction, but he was gone.

Jill still had me pinned down on the floor.

"CHARLIE!"

I saw him coming from the direction of the kitchen holding a white towel. He knelt down nearby. I knew that at any moment he was going to press the cool, clean towel gently against my face to wipe the blood away.

But that's not what he did. Carefully, very carefully, Charlie began to wipe the blood off the red carpet.

That did it. *"All he cares about is his goddam rug!"* I thought. Then, *"I've got to get out of here."*

I played possum for a minute. Then, with an extra little surge of strength, I rolled out from under Jill, sprang to my feet, snatched my glasses from the floor and ran out of there.

I got into my car and took off down the hill. The rest of Charlie's paintings were still neatly stacked in the back seat.

I drove home crying. At a stop sign, I angled the rearview mirror so I could see my face. It was a mess. There were ugly scratches on my cheeks, temples and forehead that were still bleeding.

The first thing I did when I got home was call my lawyer, Simon Taub. I told him about the scratches on my face.

"Photograph them," he said. "You never know."

The next day I had the housekeeper take Polaroids of my face, and then I filed a lawsuit against Jill Ireland for assault. That hit the tabloids: "Jill Ireland Charged with Assault."

The case was heard a few weeks later by the District Attorney in his offices on Purdue Avenue in West Los Angeles. It was a hearing to determine if I even had a case.

Still healing from my scratches, I took my girlfriend Berne along with me for emotional support. We sat in straight chairs across the desk from the DA. I was clutching the photos: *Exhibit A.*

Jill *(Mrs.* McCallum I kept calling her) looked prim as Mary Poppins in a tailored suit. She sat on a couch next to Charlie who, as always, looked angry.

The DA asked me to explain what happened. I did. Then it was Jill's turn.

In her demure style, she began to weave an entirely unfamiliar tale, the gist of which was that *I* had instigated the fight. *I* had attacked her first out of "jealousy." And she had only "defended" herself. She threw in (as she would continue to do up until the day she died) the idea that I was an unfit mother, which was a total non sequitur in this situation since we weren't there for reasons having to do with the children.

That wasn't the worst of it. When Jill finished and it was Charlie's turn, he went on to repeat, like a parrot, everything Jill had just said -- that I had instigated the fight; had attacked Jill first out of jealousy; and that Jill had only defended herself.

I was flabbergasted. Where was justice here? I might have expected Jill to lie in court, but Charlie? The old Charlie would never have done such a thing. But this wasn't the old Charlie. This was the new Charlie. This was Mr. Famous.

After Charlie and Jill left the room, the District Attorney took me aside. He told me that he believed my story, but since Charlie was the only witness, no jury would believe me. Therefore, in his view, I had no case.

Some months later, I returned the rest of the paintings to Charlie.

## Chapter 29
## The Ex Mrs. Famous

In the end it was my idea that we go through with the divorce. When the deed was done (by now it was 1965), it left a big hole in my heart.

And once the divorce was official, then everybody else was free to make their moves: David divorced Jill. Charlie married Jill. David married somebody named Kathy. Charlie and Jill had a baby girl named Zuleika. And I was alone -- as in *"The cheese stands..."*

As happens in so many divorces, friends pick sides. Most of the couples we knew went with Charlie and Jill, so I had to make new friends -- especially women friends, which wasn't always easy for me. Married women don't always welcome a single woman into their homes. Perhaps the single or divorced woman is seen as a threat or as a "fifth wheel" nuisance, but instead of dinner party invitations I was getting lots of "let's do lunch" invitations. That was fine. I did the lunches and over the years I've made and maintained some wonderful friendships with women that I value to this day

I started dating again.

What I discovered was that even if a woman has been married to a famous man for fifteen minutes, it still brands her for life. She is forevermore the woman who "used to be married to (fill in the blank)."

Some of the men I went out with were intrigued by the idea that I used to be married to Charles Bronson -- and this was years before the first *Death Wish* came out and put him over the top as a "bankable star." Being the ex Mrs. Famous gave me a dash of glamour and dating me raised the man's status a notch. Some men weren't even subtle about it. They'd introduce me as, "This is Harriett Bronson. She used to be married to Charles Bronson."

Not only is fame addictive, but marriage to fame is also addictive. It's something one gets used to and once you have it, you want more of it. I learned I wasn't alone in this view when I attended a few meetings of a kind of support group in Los Angeles called *The Ladies* (which stands for "Life after Divorce Is Eventually Sane"). I don't know if the group still exists, but it was made up of women who "used to be married to" a Mr. Famous and now needed to recover from the experience.

I also learned during this time that having been married to a famous man made me more attractive to *other* famous men. I dated a string of them. For a while I was going out with Bill Stout, a local Los Angeles news anchor who went on to become a newscaster on CBS Network News with Walter Cronkite. Though Bill I was exposed to a whole new world. I was used to actors and their fantasy world of movies and TV, but now I was in the real world and meeting and mingling with news men and women who were reporting on what was happening all around us every day. Off-camera they were smart and most had great humor. Bill told me he had a packed suitcase in the trunk of his car in case he had to leave town on a news-breaking story. One night he told me he was leaving town on an assignment. "I might have to be gone as long as *two weeks,*" he said apologetically. "Do you think you'll be okay here alone?"

I laughed. For someone who was used to separations that lasted months, two weeks was child's play.

Another man I dated was a rugged and fairly well-known actor. As luck would have it, he and Charlie ended up being in a movie together. In the movie, my actor friend had a line where his character had to say to Charlie's character, *"I saw your ex-wife last night at the club she works in."* Charlie's character then says, *"Yeah?"* Then my friend's character says, *"She has great tits,"* at which point Charlie's character socks him in the ribs. During the filming of this scene, Charlie actually broke one of my actor friend's ribs. When I asked him if he'd ever told Charlie he knew me, he said, "Are you kidding?"

Only in Hollywood!

I fell in love a few times, but after spending so many years focusing on Charlie -- on Charlie's needs, Charlie's wants, Charlie's views and on Charlie's career, I needed to avoid getting caught up in that kind of lifestyle again. To my delight, I found that most men I dated were caring and supportive and fun. It was a relief to be truly liked.

Besides, my hands were full with the children and putting my life back together. More and more, I began to see that the real world was far more interesting than the world of make-believe. I didn't know it at the time, but the experiences I was having as a single woman were actually preparing me for my eventual career in "talk radio." But that was still a few years down the road.

Chapter 30
Motherhood on Trial

It's always something.

Initially, Charlie and I had joint custody of the children and we were able to work cooperatively with this situation. Divorced couples have to stay in each other's lives. You divorced each *other*, not the kids. That means you work with it. And we did just that.

We shared every other holiday and Charlie was always free to be with the children any weekend he was in town. During summers they traveled to Charlie's farm in Vermont. There were even times when Tony and Suzanne went on movie locations with him. If it happened to be during the school year, they'd be accompanied by tutors. (The studios were paying for it now that Charlie was a star.)

True, these arrangements were complex and far from perfect, but under the circumstances they worked. We both did the best we could to meet the children's physical, educational and emotional needs which, after all, was the whole point.

But then, in 1971, our comfortable agreement to get along because of the children changed and we found ourselves engaged in a huge court battle over physical custody of Tony. (Suzanne was already sixteen and legally could make up her own mind). It was a case during which Jill, once again, deliberately told lies to paint a picture of me as a bad mother.

This was a particularly painful charge for me because I was already full of self-doubts in this area. Since my mother had died before I was even three and I had no siblings, I had no role-models for mothering. With my own kids I was never sure if what I was doing was "good enough." I felt a tremendous responsibility to make everything "right" for them, causing Charlie to constantly call me a "worry wart."

Charlie, on the other hand, had his mother and all those siblings so for him being a parent was a breeze.

Nevertheless, in spite of our parenting differences, things felt in balance -- until Charlie more and more seemed to fall under Jill's influence. I began to suspect he was *intimidated* by her. Instead of viewing me as just a "worry wart," he was now interpreting my mothering style in a very negative light. This made me feel betrayed by him all over again. It was hard to take.

There was a whole back-story of events leading up to this 1971 court battle: During the time of my "walking nervous breakdown" after our divorce, when I knew I had to get myself back together emotionally, I'd asked Charlie if he and Jill would consider having Tony and Suzanne stay with them for two years while I got my life organized. I had just sold the house and wanted to look for an apartment. They'd agreed. I got the apartment, and the kids stayed there with me on weekends as well as when Charlie and Jill were on location, which was often.

This plan worked until Tony became terrified of one of the servants in Charlie's and Jill's household, a man they'd hired as a caretaker to make sure things ran smoothly when they were out of town. The man was verbally abusive to Tony (but not to Suzanne), and Tony was scared of him. I called Charlie in London and told him what was going on. I informed him that I was going to remove Tony from the house to get him away from this man.

Charlie, instead of focusing on what was happening to Tony, accused me of "causing trouble" and refused to believe the facts as I knew them. He threatened to call the police if I took Tony out of the house.

I refused to let Charlie's threats stop me. I went to the house, threw Tony's clothes into a big box -- with everyone in the household looking on in astonishment -- and yanked Tony out of there. When Charlie and Jill returned home to Los Angeles, I wouldn't let Tony go back to them.

At that point, Charlie decided he not only wanted Tony to move back in for the remainder of our two-year agreement, but *forever*. What he and Jill didn't bother to tell me was that after they'd returned from Europe, they'd realized I was right about the caretaker, so they'd fired him. Since I didn't know that, I decided there was no way I was going to allow Tony to move back into that house, so we ended up in court.

Again, I had no witnesses. Charlie had several, including a publicist's assistant (I'd never met her; didn't even know who she was), a woman who stated with great certainty on the witness stand that I had given up my children for "an acting career." My attorney, Simon Taub, cross-examined her: Was she a friend of Jill's? She said yes. Had she ever been to Jill's house? She said no. When he asked her how she knew about this case, she said she'd read about it in the trades (the industry newspapers). My attorney thanked her, said he had no further questions, and she was dismissed.

When Jill was on the witness stand, the judge asked her if I was a good mother. She said "*No.*" Then Charlie took the stand and said that he and Jill provided a better place for Tony to live.

Next, the judge asked me to tell my whole story, which I did, adding that I intended to devote my life to completing the job of raising, loving and caring for Tony and Suzanne.

In the end, the judge talked to Tony privately in his chambers. Later, the judge told me never to ask Tony what he'd told the judge. He said to Charlie, "You may have a *house* for Tony, but my judgment is you don't have a *home*. Therefore, I am awarding physical custody of Tony to his mother; joint custody to you both, as outlined in the 1965 divorce decree, as well as visitation rights to the father, Charles Bronson."

Suzanne later assured me that while she loved me, she preferred all the activities and opportunities that were available to her at Charlie's and Jill's house, so she opted to remain living with them – which she did until she was seventeen and moved out on her own. I could understand her choice. For a young girl, it probably was a lot more exciting at Charlie's house than at my apartment. We've been able to maintain a good relationship with each other ever since.

My feelings where Charlie was concerned were raw. I still felt short-changed by him because I didn't get "my turn." Now that the children were once again going back and forth between homes, I noticed that Jill not only didn't iron shirts, but she had a laundress as well as nannies, cooks, and a butler -- the works. I'd guess I'd have liked living there, too. I also noticed that Charlie no longer seemed to be complaining that it was like "Grand Central Station" there.

I came to the conclusion that it's the *second* wife, or even the third, who gets all the perks. When Charlie and Jill went on vacation, they took an entourage of helpers along. And then there was that business of Charlie putting Jill in some of his movies. Another of my dreams for myself gone awry; another reminder of what *might* have been.

Yes, it was definitely time for me to kick-start my own life.

## Chapter 31
## Taking My Turn

It took me seven years to reclaim "the real Harriett Bronson." It sounded like a fine idea, but when it came to taking concrete actions, I didn't know where to start.

I made an appointment with Dr. Sanderson, my favorite psychologist, for a therapy tune-up. It had been a while.

"When you were a kid what did you want to be when you grew up?" he asked me.

"An actress."

"What happened?"

"I met Charlie."

"You changed horses in mid-stream."

"I did."

"So change back."

"And do what?"

"That's for you to figure out," he said. "Try things. See what clicks."

And try things I did. I met a man by the name of Buddy Garion who talked me into joining an acting class taught by choreographer and actor, Steven Peck, 40's, a well-built former dancer with New York street good looks. He was sitting in a director's chair when I arrived in his class in Beverly Hills, an L.A. area phone book in his lap. He was surrounded by a dozen fresh-faced acting students, sitting in a circle. Aside from Peck, I was the oldest person in the room.

"You're Harriett Bronson?" he asked.

"Yes."

Then came the inevitable question: "Any relation to the actor?"

"Ex wife," I said.

"The man's a damn fool!" Peck said, standing up. He gave me a hug and welcomed me into their fold.

When I sat down he handed me the phone book.

"What's this for?" I asked.

"It's your scene book."

"You're joking."

There was giggling from the other students. "No he's not," said one.

"Quiet or I'll break your legs," Steve Peck said. He liked to play up his lower East Side, Mafia-in-the-family roots with occasional mobster jokes.

He went on. "Okay, doll, open it up and read a name."

I opened the phone book.

"Roland I. Miller," I read.

"Address and phone number, too."

I gave him an "Are you crazy?" look.

"Go ahead."

"11527 Ventura Boulevard. 820-6003."

"Any more Millers?"

"Yes. Like a hundred of them."

"Go down the list of Millers, but read 'em happy."

"Happy?"

"Happy."

"How can I do that? It's just a list of names and numbers."

"You went to drama school, didn't you? That's what your friend Buddy told me."

"A million years ago."

"It's like riding a bicycle. Go on."

I decided to dive in. Adding a lilt to my voice and a smile, along with some up-beat body movements, I read the next dozens Millers in the phone book "happy."

"Now read 'em angry."

I did that -- until I got to one name, *Samuel* Miller. Then I choked up.

"What just happened there?" Peck asked.

"Samuel's my father's name. He's been very ill. The name reminded me. I miss him." I felt tears come to my eyes.

Steve Peck and the students remained silent.

Peck broke the silence. "So, what did you learn today about acting from reading the phone book?"

"Whoever wrote it is one hell of a good writer!"

The class burst into laughter.

I was completely surprised. I grinned wider than I had in years.

"So you said something funny and people laughed," Dr. Sanderson said during our next therapy session when told him about the acting class.

"I wouldn't have dared opened my mouth if Charlie had been there. He's have thought it was stupid."

"Are you going back to the class?"

"It's what I was trained to do – but I don't know if acting is still what I *want* to do."

"It doesn't have to be acting."

I did go back to Steven Peck's class, mostly because I didn't yet know what else to do, and I'm glad I did. By being there, my self-esteem slowly began to come back. Steven filmed me doing a couple of scenes and encouraged me to show them to some agents and producers, which I did. I figured I would give my acting ability a chance. I was also put in contact with a publicist and was eventually signed by the Hal Schaffer Agency as "Dena" Bronson, as well as by a commercial agency, Pacific Artists, as "Harriett Bronson."

Obviously, I still couldn't quite decide who I was!

One day while house cleaning I came across a book I used to read to Tony called *No Dessert Until You Finish Your Mashed Potatoes*. It was a humorous take on a child's view of his mother. It gave me the idea of writing a humor book from the mother's point of view about her children. I called it, *Shut Up, I'm on the Phone*. I made contact with Larry Sloan of Price/Stern/Sloan Publishers. He not only published this book but another one I wrote about real estate called, *Do I Have a House for You*.

I also discovered another talent. Or *re*-discovered it, I should say. I had a *talent for spotting talent*. I'd done it years earlier when I'd seen Charlie "in my mind's eye" as a movie star. But until now I'd never appreciated that being able to spot talent *is* a talent.

I met a pretty young song writer, Judy Hinger, who impressed me with her song-writing abilities. I listened to the professional demos she'd had made and I thought they were terrific. Even though I had no connections to anyone in the music business, I made up a job for myself as Judy's "personal manager" and "song plugger," and I started representing her. This led to discovering another talent: I'm good at selling on the phone – not selling myself, but selling others. I approached some music publishers who represented major recording artists, asked them to listen to Judy Hinger's demos, and I ended up getting eleven of her songs published and recorded by major recording stars. I even used one of her songs as my theme song years later on one of my radio shows.

I surprised myself.

I later represented a couple of "How To" book authors, as well as my therapist friend (the one who'd enlightened me about jealousy), who was also a writer. I put her together with a publisher I knew and he published three of her books. And I represented another friend who'd invented a board game.

But I still felt I hadn't found "it" – whatever "it" was. My mission. My passion. My calling.

So I kept looking.

Then, in 1971, I met a man who, to this day, does not know that he changed the course of my life. I was visiting a friend at a local Los Angeles TV station. Upon leaving, I had a chance encounter with none other than Regis Philbin who was co-hosting a local newsy televison show with Stan Boreman. I introduced myself and mentioned how much I enjoyed his TV show. He told me he was on his way over to KABC to do a *radio* show.

"Are you also disc jockey?" I asked.

He laughed. "No, it's *talk* radio."

"Talk radio?"

"Yeah, you should listen to it."

I decided to check out this thing called "talk radio."

Call it serendipity, but *listening to the radio* -- which had so long ago been my solace on those lonely nights on the farm -- now became my salvation. Amazingly enough, years later I was a guest on Regis Philbin's *A.M. Los Angeles* Show after my two humor books were published.

Not only did I became an avid listener of "talk radio" but I also became an avid caller. I called in constantly.

One of my favorite talk shows was the *Ken Minyard Show* on KABC in Los Angeles. It was on every week day. I'd listen when I went to pick up Tony from school. Ken Minyard discussed things that were right up my alley.

For example, one day I got into my car to go pick up Tony and Minyard was talking about infidelity – a subject I knew more than a little about:

*Ken Minyard: Here's the situation. Say a happily married woman's husband cheats on her but she doesn't know it. If she finds out, does that negate all those years she had with him when she thought she was happy? We want to know what you think. Give us a call...*

The minute I got home and got Tony settled down at the kitchen table to do his homework, I slipped into the bedroom and called in to KABC. I was put through:

*Me: Earlier today you asked if a happily married woman's husband cheats on her and then she finds out about it, does it negate all those years she thought she was happy —*

*Minyard: And what's your answer?*

*Me: My answer is no, it doesn't negate all those years she thought she was happy. Just like if you go to a restaurant and have a lovely meal and then later get food poisoning, does that mean you didn't enjoy the meal?*

*Minyard:  Unless the meal kills you.*

*Me:  But you still enjoyed the meal.*

He laughed.

Minyard: *What's your name?*

I didn't expect that.

*Me: Debra.*

*Minyard: Thanks, Debra, interesting take on the situation.*

The infidelity topic was a popular one. It came up a lot on Ken's show. And I always called in as "Debra" to shoot my mouth off.

*Minyard: Why do you think men cheat, Debra?*

*Me: Because they can. But I have the solution. What if all single women refused to have anything to do with married men? A boycott. The men would be forced to either work out their issues with their wives, or get divorced. No trying to have it both ways. No trying to have your cake and eat it, too.*

*Minyard: Another unique idea from Debra. Thanks, Debra.*

One afternoon I was listening to Ken Minyard while I was cooking dinner. It's hard to imagine this situation today, but they were debating whether or not the employment want-ads in the *Los Angeles Times* should continue to be segregated into Help Wanted: Male and Help Wanted: Female:

*Minyard: That was Libby from the National Organization for Women calling in to say that she thinks newspaper help-wanted ads should be desegregated. Call in and tell us what you think? Segregated or combined? Call us at 1-800-KABC.*

I grabbed for the phone and dialed. As I was waiting to get through, a woman was telling Ken she thought men and woman have different capabilities and therefore the want-ads shouldn't be desegregated. I finally got on the air.

*Me: I don't believe that woman actually said that!*

*Minyard: Give us your name.*

*Me: Debra again.*

*Minyard: You're getting to be a regular. Okay, Debra, what's on your mind?*

*Me: That woman who just called in, she's got it all wrong, completely wrong --*

As I launched into my diatribe on the subject, I realized that sounding off felt good. Maybe it was because of Charlie's "stupid" remarks, but I felt a freedom in speaking my mind while hiding behind a pseudonym.

A week later I was back on the air. This time Ken Minyard recognized my voice, which he told me was "sexy." It felt good to have a man give me a compliment. I needed it.

Three or four times a week for the next eight or nine months, the phone receiver cradled under my chin, I'd call the *Ken Minyard Show,* as the mysterious Debra, while I cooked dinner or folded the laundry.

One afternoon I tuned in to the show while driving home from the market:

*Minyard: Welcome to the Ken Minyard Show. Today we have good news and bad news. The good news is we have a great show lined up for you; the bad news is it's our last show.*

Out loud I said, "Oh, no!"

When I got home, I called the show's producer, Pam Gentry, and made an appointment to come in.

The next day at KABC I found myself sitting across the desk from the Program Director, Jim Simon.

"What can I do for you?"

"I came down to find out why you're taking Ken Minyard off the air?"

"Ratings," he said.

"But he's the best thing on radio."

"He may be, but he doesn't have the numbers. He's going to be doing the morning drive show instead."

He interrupted himself. "Excuse me, but your voice sounds familiar. Have we talked before?"

"I'm Debra. I've been calling in to the *Ken Minyard Show* for the past year."

"Of course! You're our star caller. But that's not the name you just gave the receptionist."

"Harriett Bronson."

Then came *that* question: "Any relation to the actor?"

"Ex wife," I said. "I'm the ex Mrs. Famous." I was itching to get back to the subject. "Can't you fix Ken's show"

"Any ideas?"

I wasn't prepared for that question.

"All I know is how I'd do it if I were hosting the show."

"How would that be?"

"I'd have on non-celebrity guests and pick their brains -- people who are doing unusual things but nobody ever hears about them because all the other radio shows only interview celebrities."

"Can you give me an example?"

Another question I wasn't prepared for.

"Did you ever see the Singing Flower Man at the Century City Mall? Every time I'm at the mall I wonder what his story is. He's practically a landmark. But does anybody know anything about him? Wouldn't you like to know how he ended up being a Singing Flower Man? Ken could have him on and interview him and find out."

"What else?"

"Have you got an hour?"

"I'll tell you what Debra -- Harriett, if you have time, I'll take you down the hall to the conference room and sit you at a table with a pad of paper and maybe you can write down some of your ideas. We'll look them over and give you a call."

"Sure." What did I have to lose? "Do you think it'll help save Ken's show?"

"I can't promise anything. All I can do is say we'll try."

The next day Jim Simon called me as I was doing the laundry.

"Harriett? Jim Simon at KABC."

My mind was on dirty socks.

"Did I catch you at a bad time?"

"I was just doing the laundry."

"Look, I went over your ideas with my boss and he was impressed, but unfortunately we're not going to be able to save Ken's show. The numbers just aren't there."

"I was afraid of that. Anyway, thanks for telling me."

"Wait! Hold on! We're working on an idea for another show."

"Yes, you said – Ken's drive time show."

"No. *Your* show. The Debra Show."

I sat down on a pile of sheets.

"We've got a time slot open Sunday afternoons from three to five. We'd like to give you a try."

"I'm not a professional radio person. I'm just a wanna-be-has-been actress."

"That's the whole point," Jim Simon said. "It'll be a talk show hosted by a former caller with some fresh ideas. We think it's a cute gimmick. You've got that great husky voice and the listeners already know you."

"Shouldn't I be starting out in the mail room or something?"

"Line up some of those non-celebrity guests; show up next Sunday by two and I'll sit down with you and show you the ropes."

Then he added, "Just be yourself."

I laughed. "I have no idea who that is. That's why I'm seeing a therapist."

The next day I called my favorite Beverly Hills Detective, Kip Ameritti, the one I'd hired (and my father had paid) to follow Charlie. I invited him to be on my first show. I spent hours making obsessive preparations. My kitchen table was cluttered with notes, newspapers, magazines, address books, phone books and library books.

Sunday came and I arrived at KABC a nervous wreck. Jim Simon led me into a small studio and sat me down. He sat down next to me. He assured me that someone would be in-studio with me for a few weeks to help me work "the log"—commercials, callers, traffic reports. After that I'd be on my own.

"It looks like the Houston Space Center in here. What do I push?"

"The technician will take care of all that. All you have to do is talk."

The music started. The engineer behind the glass gave me some kind of signal.

"What's *that* mean?"

"That's the "On the Air" signal."

"On the air!"

"Just talk."

Jim pointed to the microphone. "Speak."

"Speak?"

"Yes. "

Nervously, I checked my script and then -- just like Clark Kent in the phone booth turning into Superman -- when Jim Simon clicked the microphone to "ON," my acting classes came back to me and I was calm. I automatically lowered my voice to what he later told me was "all purr" and I began.

*Harriett: Hi, I'm Debra and welcome to KABC and my new show, the Debra Show. If some of you recognize my voice, it's because you've heard it before -- not as a talk show host but as a caller. Yes, I'm the Debra who's been calling in to the Ken Maynard Show for the past year. Well, now here I am -- and I hope you like my show.*

I looked over at Jim Simon. He winked and gave me an A-OK sign.

I smiled at Kip who was now sitting across the desk from me. I could see that he was experiencing a little stage fright. I patted his hand reassuringly. I continued:

*Harriett: Today my in-studio guest is Beverly Hills detective Kip Ameritti. His specialty is following wayward husbands and wives. Welcome, Detective. You're in a pretty hazardous profession, aren't you? Tell me, has an angry husband ever taken a swipe at you?*

*Kip Ameritti: It has happened. In fact, a few years ago I was following a famous movie star, who shall remain nameless, and when I caught up with him and the lady in question, he punched me out pretty good. I had a sore jaw for a week. And I've been dining out on that story ever since.*

We laughed.

When we broke for a commercial, Jim Simon asked me, "Well, how do you like the job so far?"

"I like it a lot."

The next two hours flew by. When it was over I was jazzed. "Is it over so soon?"

I couldn't wait until the following Sunday.

I knew I had found my calling. I was home.

I was to end up doing talk radio for a total of nine years. On KABC, I was initially on the air on Sundays from three to five in the afternoon. Then I was on Sunday nights from midnight to five. On KIEV, I also had the Sunday midnight to five shift. When I was on KGIL, it was daytimes from ten a.m. until two in the afternoon.

Basically, my shows, no matter where I did them, were always the same. They were all about lifestyles, human behavior and the entertainment industry, with guests who had expertise in these areas but weren't themselves famous.

I billed myself as a "conversationalist," an expert "only on my own personal life experience." Sometimes I did the show alone and threw out topics – such as a show on cults and another on the Fat Underground. The only requirement for being on my show was having something of interest to say.

I guess, in a way, that's what I always wanted for myself.

On KIEV, when I did the night shift. I'd get up to eighty calls a night from night owls and we'd talk about everything -- divorce, aggression, separate bedrooms, movies. I loved it.

In fact, I was crazy about talk radio.

And doing a radio show definitely had its perks. I was given tickets to every major theatre production in Los Angeles. Best seats in the house. I was invited to book parties and movie screenings. I was on discussion panels about talk-radio. Five hundred people showed up at a screening at 20th Century Fox where I made a personal appearance and gave a greeting before the movie. Photos were taken; autographs signed.

Another personal appearance at Myron's Ballroom drew one thousand fans of my show. And there were other appearances at my sponsor's restaurant, Junior's Deli in Westwood, where people were lined up around the block.

I received a ton of fan mail requesting photos. I autographed every photo and personally mailed them out myself.

I was most certainly getting "my turn!"


It wasn't until many years later that I learned that I'd become a kind of folk hero to my younger cousins back home in Philadelphia. Their parents would tell them stories about how their cousin Harriett -- against all odds – had left home in 1949 to marry a poor Lithuanian former coal miner who wasn't even Jewish, but had a dream and followed it. They marveled at what Charlie Buchinsky had become. *Death Wish* really made that point in a big way.

Running away in order to follow your dream just wasn't done in those days, so Charlie and I were held up as examples of what is possible.

# BRONSON FAMILY ALBUM
## PART 3

Me with Tony, age 4,
after Charlie left

Los Angeles, California, with Tony and Suzanne, mid-1970's

Suzanne and Tony on a Mother's Day

I couldn't even go into a supermarket without seeing FAN MAGAZINES with headlines like: "NEW LOVE CRISIS FOR McCALLUM as Wife Faces Assault Charge;"..."The Man Waiting for the McCallums to Divorce Says, 'We Don't' Want to Hurt Him'"..."The Night David McCallum's Wife Forgot She Was Married!" I tortured myself by buying -- and reading -- them all!

My Life in the 1960's in Fan Magazines

## OK, So Who Am I?

After Charlie and I got divorced, I spent years trying to get myself back on a career path, starting with acting, using two different names, Dena Bronson and Harriett Bronson.

## But -- IS ACTING REALLY IT?

I also tried commercial
work, but wondered...
IS COMMERCIAL
WORK REALLY IT?

Dick Heffernam Personal Management

(Right) And for fun, a little
dressing up for an Easter
Seals Foundation Costume
Ball in the 1970's.

# IS WRITING REALLY IT?

(Above) Here I am on the *A.M. Los Angeles Show*
with Regis Philbin, publicizing one of my humor
books, "Have I Got a House for You!"

**HARRIETT BRONSON**                    **KIEV RADIO .87 AM**

In the 1970s, after trying acting, voice-overs and a bunch of other things, I finally returned to my first love as far back as High School -- RADIO. By a fluke (plus what my father always called my "fierce determination"), I landed a spot on a talk radio show. After I got over my terror, I loved it and even got pretty good at it. I did "talk radio" for a total of nine years.

Photos by Charles Killeen

DEBRA                    **KABC TALKRADIO 79** ⓐⓑⓒ

Here I am on KABC as "Debra" and then on KIEV as myself.

Photos: Charles Killeen

We get (fan) mail! (KIEV RADIO)

Delmar Watson Photography

(Left) I am given a high compliment when a cover story article appears in the Los Angeles Daily News, calling me the "Best Female Voice in Radio." Below, left – My Dating Years – Here in 1979 with Charles Killeen, who took some of the photos of me doing talk radio shows. Below, right – another favorite companion, my miniature dachshund, Luci Noel, 1980.

2000 – Photo of me with my cousins on my mother's side of the family. (Left to right): Joe Fenkel, me, Fran Blum and Bill Fenkel. The occasion was the wedding of Fran's daughter, Katie. (Fran was named after my mother, Frances, her aunt. Katie was named after our grandmother, Gram Katie) .

Photo by David LaPorte

(Below) 1999: Me with my escort, Buddy Garion, at my daughter Suzanne's wedding.

(Above) Snap Shots from the Present. (Below) My Friends, "The Magnificant Seven" (Left to right) Estra Schaffer, Judy Savar, Me, Joanne Wanderman, Debby Berg, Shaela Pollock and Sylvia Cary.

Photo below by David LaPorte

## Chapter 32
### Woman to Woman

In 1984 Jill Ireland was diagnosed with breast cancer. It looked bad. Then she had a remission and wrote a book, *Life Wish*, which was about her illness and recovery. It became a best-seller. In fact, the book brought her more fame than she'd ever had as an actress, or as Charles Bronson's wife.

I'd had a great deal of anger at Jill for her part in the upheaval in my life, and for her on-going assaults on my reputation as a mother by continually telling the media that she had "raised seven children" when *two* of those children just happened to be mine. *She* hadn't raised them, *I'd* raised them. That really irked me. But this new battle that she was now facing transcended all that. As one woman to another, I felt badly for her. I also came to deeply admire her for her fierce determination to overcome obstacles -- a trait that we both had in common.

Jill did everything anybody could do to heal herself, and I respected her for it. Plus she spoke out publicly, which I'm sure was comforting to many other women going through the same experience. So a few months after she got home from the hospital, I called her. I'd heard about a clinic in Germany that was doing some unique things for cancer patients and I wanted to tell her about it.

"I wish you'd tell Charlie," she said. "Maybe if he hears it from you he'll listen."

I found that remark strange. Had they been disagreeing over various ways to deal with her illness?

Before I could stop her, she put Charlie on the phone. I knew in my gut it was a mistake. I was right.

"Why are you doing this, Harriett?" Charlie barked at me. "What's it to *you?* Why do you even *care?* Butt out!"

Twenty years suddenly dropped away like a veil. Same old Charlie, still angry and suspicious after all these years.

"I don't want to see her die," I said.

"Yeah, right." He hung up.

It wasn't all altruism on my part. Charlie was right about that but for the wrong reason. I had plenty of selfish reasons for not wanting Jill to die. After years of turmoil and animosity, we had all finally adjusted. Suzanne and Tony were fond of Jill and had become accustomed to two different families with two different lifestyles -- ours rather simple, Charlie's and Jill's rather lavish. My family was feeling intact. Charlie's family was intact.

Everything, for once, was going smoothly. I wanted it to stay that way.

## Chapter 33
## Saying Goodbyes

One evening I got a call. The first thing that flashed through my head was "Jill," but the call wasn't about Jill. Charlie's brother, Dempsey, had just died.

I arrived at the grave site with Tony and Suzanne.

Jill was sitting in a chair, looking frail. She was wearing a fashionable black and white dress with a black hat and white hatband. Their daughter, Zuleika, was there also, as were Jill's sons Paul and Val, as well as Katrina (whom they raised) and Jill's adopted son, Jason, whose own funeral (he died of a drug overdose) Jill would attend only a few years later.

Catherine was there with her husband, Joseph. Next to them were Hollywood Joe and Jennie; Anne (Dempsey's widow), some family friends, and Charlie.

The priest had just finished speaking. The male relatives stood and placed their boutonnieres on Dempsey's casket.

Afterwards, while everyone was still standing around, Charlie broke away from Jill and his group and walked over to me. He took me into his arms and gave me a long, tight hug.

"I guess this means I'm next," he whispered in my ear.

I was completely astounded. Everyone was watching us. Tony was visibly upset. He'd never seen his father touch me, and didn't know what to make of it. He'd been so young when Charlie and I had separated that he had no recollection of Charlie ever living in the house with us. He interpreted this hug as romantic.

"Mom, remember my father is married to Jill," he said to me under his breath.

In that moment, I felt sorry for Charlie. He seemed so strong to everybody else, but I knew he was grieving. I also realized that today he didn't even have to strength to be angry with me. He knew I'd always been fond of Dempsey, and I think he was grateful that I was there.

"Bring Suzanne and Tony back to the house for the reception" he said. I didn't expect this either.

"Is it okay with Jill?"

"Jill's the one who told me to ask you."

"We'll be there."


Half an hour later Suzanne, Tony and I drove up to Charlie's and Jill's sprawling, 35-room Mediterranean-style mansion on the 18th hole of the Bel Air Golf Club. As we drove past the guard gate with the 24-hour guard, I thought of a story I'd once heard about a Charles Bronson look-alike from the Ron Smith Celebrity Look-Alike Agency who'd managed to get by both the guard and the gardener -- and walk right up to the front door before somebody had finally stopped him.

When we arrived at the entrance, we were met by a swarm of valet parking attendants. I relinquished the car we went inside.

Jill was standing by the heavy wood-carved front door wearing a blond wig.

"Hello, Harriett dear."

"Hello, Jill. Your house is lovely."

"Thank you, dear. We like it. There's food in there."

Jill embraced Suzanne and Tony.

"Zuleika just went down to the stables if you want to join her, Suzanne. Tony, there's a young lady inside perhaps you'd like to meet."

As Suzanne and Tony disappeared, I moved into the living room and looked around. It was furnished with antiques from all over the world -- oriental rugs, stained glass windows and a winding staircase right out of an English movie.

Over the mantle there was a huge painting of Jill -- in jodhpurs -- on horseback.

When I saw my ex sister-in-law, Jennie, Hollywood Joe's wife, I went over to her. We embraced. "It's good to see you," I said. "I'm so sorry about Dempsey. He was always a favorite of mine."

We perched ourselves on the window seat in front of a large picture window overlooking the lush green sweep of the Bel Air golf course.

"What a view," I said.

"A little different than the view of the outhouse and the No. 8 coal mine back in Scooptown."

I laughed. "Scooptown had a certain quaint charm. I'll never forget my first visit there after Charlie and I got engaged. The whole family was so nice to me."

Jennie laughed. "Don't you remember what my son Terry said about that? He said, 'Of *course* the family was nice to her. Charlie was bringing home a princess!'"

We both laughed, then sat back to watch Charlie being the perfect host. When a guest spilled a drink, Charlie dabbed at the spill with a napkin to mop it up.

"He's still a neat freak," Jennie said.

Charlie walked over to us. "You gals want any soda pop?"

I shook my head.

"Not for me," Jennie said.

"Jill looks well," I said.

"She's come through this thing like a thoroughbred. Chemo's rough. You mind if Suzanne stays over? Zuleika's got a new horse."

"Just tell her to be careful."

"Worry wart. So what's new with you?"

"I'm at KIEV now."

"That so?" Charlie said, uninterested.

"Midnight to dawn. If you can't sleep, listen in."

"I sleep fine."

He still had a genius for saying things that got me right in the gut.

"I guess you could say I'm finally taking my turn."

"What's that supposed to mean?"

"By having my own radio show."

"And cashing in on my name?"

I was taken aback. I had to force myself to respond before I got rolled over again. "It's my name, too, Charlie."

Jennie, feeling the need to stand up for me, jumped in: "You should hear her. She's got a knack for drawing people out who aren't used to being interviewed. It's a real skill."

"It pays shit, I bet, right?"

After a beat to gather my thoughts, I answered: "It pays enough. I love doing it."

"Fruitcake."

Charlie's attention span had reached its limit. He reached into his jacket pocket and took out a snapshot. He handed it to me. "Look at this. It's the house I just bought in Malibu. What do you think?"

"Impressive," I said. It was. It was beautiful.

He beamed. "Paid a million bucks for it. Cash." Emphasis on the *cash*.

"You could buy Scooptown for that," Jennie exclaimed.

"You can keep Scooptown," Charlie shot back, turning to me. "Making money's the same as riding in that Cadillac we used to have. You get to like the comfort of the ride." Then he laughed, and moved on to mingle: "Soda pop anybody?"

"He sure likes the good life," I whispered to Jennie.

"Always did. Funny how we all turned out the way it looked like we were going to. Even you. Your own radio show. My-my."

"Better late than never."

I stood and picked up my purse. "I need to find the powder room. Then I've got to split to get ready for my show tonight. Back in a sec."

I climbed the elegant staircase leading up to the second floor where I looked for the bathroom. It was occupied. I walked down the hall looking for another one. I saw Charlie's and Jill's master bedroom and walked through it to the master bathroom.

On the counter in the bathroom was a tray holding dozens of prescription bottles. A dozen blonde wigs, purchased after Jill had lost her hair from rounds of chemotherapy, were on wig stands. I picked up one with long, straight blond hair -- the hairstyle Jill had been wearing the day she and I had that knock-down, drag-out fight. I tried it on. It looked awful on me. I replaced it on its stand, then, as an afterthought, I tied two long strands of wig hair in a knot. I stood back and took a good look at myself -- with some satisfaction. I was wearing a dark brown pants suit. Charlie had been right about brown – it was always my best color and brought out the color of my eyes.

On the way back downstairs, I looked down over the railing. Jill and Charlie were standing directly below me. I overheard a fragment of their conversation:

"I saw you!" I heard Charlie saying under his breath.

"You saw nothing. I was not flirting. Now shut up." Jill then turned and walked back into the living room, all smiles.

I rejoined Jennie by the huge picture window.

"Do you realize that if you hadn't divorced Charlie, all this would be yours?" she asked.

"The thought crossed my mind, but I'm afraid the price is too high."

I picked up the brown pashmina that one of my loyal girlfriends had bought for me on my birthday, hugged Jennie goodbye, and went into the dining room where I signaled to Tony who was talking with a pretty blond girl.

"Tony, I'm leaving now. You want to stay?"

He glanced at the girl. "Yeah."

Charlie was standing at the front door saying goodbye to some guests. I held out my hand.

"Thanks for coming," he said. .

"I wanted to. Take care," I said, and I left.

Outside, I walked down the stone steps and described my car to a parking attendant. He took off down the driveway towards the parking lot.

I waiting on the bottom step for him to return, but when I looked down the hill I could see that retrieving my car was going to call for maneuvering a lot of other cars first, so I climbed back up the four or five steps to the front porch and sat down on a stone bench to wait. Charlie, at the doorway, was only ten feet away talking with his guests.

It was a beautiful, warm day.

A slight breeze blew the branches of the trees and the tops of the well-tended flowers.

The misty water from a lawn sprinkler caught the sunlight and made a rainbow.

I closed my eyes and tipped my face up to the sun. I felt peaceful and calm.

"Harriett?"

I opened my eyes. I must have been starting to fall asleep.

"Harriett?"

I looked up and saw Charlie standing by the front door, looking at me.

I got up and then, just as I'd done so many decades earlier, I walked over to him as though being reeled in and stood in front of him.

"You still have the most beautiful lips I've ever seen."

"Thank you."

Jill was only yards away. I felt suddenly uncomfortable.

"I'm sorry about what I said in there about cashing in on my name. Good luck with the radio show."

"Thank you for saying that."

He gave me another intense hug. "Bye now."

"Good bye, Charlie Buchinsky."

I turned and once again went down the stone front steps of the driveway just as the parking attendant squealed up with my car. He jumped out and gallantly opened the door for me.

"Did you get to talk to Charles Bronson?" he said.

"Sure did."

"Cool."

As I drove down the long driveway past the stables, I saw Suzanne and Zuleika on horseback. I beeped my horn. They both looked up and waved. I waved back and drove on.

I tipped the rear-view mirror and saw Charlie's mansion getting smaller and smaller behind me. I drove through the huge wrought iron gates past the guard's station.

When I reached the street, I tilted the mirror back in place and turned on the radio just in time to catch my own promo:

> *Harriett (VO): Hi. I'm Harriett Bronson. Tune in tonight when I'll be with you, from midnight to five a.m. I've got a fabulous show and some great guests, so tune in and call in to KIEV and join us -- the night people.*

I fiddled with the radio knob until I found a jazz station and left it there. Then I pulled onto the freeway and merged into the flow of traffic, heading home.

## Epilogue

Jill Ireland's remission lasted a number of years, but the cancer eventually returned, spreading to her lungs and to other parts of her body. She underwent more painful months of radiation, chemotherapy and surgery. In May of 1990, she died.

Four years later, in the fall of 1994, just months after the L.A. earthquake had trashed my house, I, too, was diagnosed with breast cancer. I went through six months of chemotherapy. I lost my hair. The hair stylist, Cristophe, the man who gave President Bill Clinton his famous $200 haircut, made up a wig for me. I got more compliments on that wig than I'd ever received for my real hair. I was even a little disappointed when my own hair started growing back in again. My one compensation was that it grew back curly.

Suzanne told me that when Charlie was told about my illness, he said, in total seriousness, *"All* women get breast cancer."

Charlie never once phoned me to see how I was doing, never even sent a get well card. That thawing-out at Dempsey's funeral was short-lived. He was mad at me for ending our marriage and he couldn't forgive. If there was one thing Charlie Bronson was, it was resolute.

As far as my breast cancer goes, as of this writing it has been sixteen years since my diagnosis and treatment and, fingers crossed, I seem to be okay.

The last time I saw Charlie alive (he was then 77) was at our daughter Suzanne's wedding in 1999. There was some drama leading up to this event. Initially, the plan was for Suzanne to be married at his house. But Charlie himself had married again and he didn't want me to attend – my own daughter's wedding! I had let many things slide to keep the peace, but this time I made a fuss. I threatened to go public unless Charlie held the wedding at a hotel so I could be there. And he did. It took place at the gorgeous Bel Air Hotel.

The tabloids actually wrote a very nice story about the wedding, which I ended up attending with a date, my old friend Buddy Garion, and wearing a very expensive new dress. Charlie gave me a lingering hug when he saw me just before the ceremony, and then he danced with me, in front of everybody -- for the last time.

I wasn't the only one present that day who felt that Charlie seemed slightly "out of it" and "distracted." I have no way of knowing this for sure, but his demeanor might have been a hint of an affliction he was said to be hit with later -- Alzheimer's.

In the years following Suzanne's wedding, I got blindsided with a string of disasters: Lung cancer in 2001; a broken femur in 2002 and, thanks to the fact that the metal plate that was put in my leg also broke, a second leg surgery in 2002 -- resulting in a total of seven and a half months spent in a physical rehabilitation hospital.

That fierce determination that my father (who died shortly after that illness I mentioned in Steven Peck's acting class) used to chide me about, now pulled me through once again. I had a laser focus on my treatment and recovery, and am now, as of my latest tests, cancer free and walking again. But I must admit I am not crazy about this aging process.

I enjoyed watching Charlie's incredible success, even after I was no longer a part of it. At least the children were a part of it, and for them it was wonderful. From having four cents in his pocket, the fact that he went on to become one of the most famous and highest paid actors in the world is amazing. Just witnessing all that was a trip. Basically, I think Charlie was satisfied with his life in spite of a few regrets. He got where he wanted to go. And since reaching the goal isn't as important as the process, I hope he enjoyed the process. I think he did.

And Charlie was right. I *did* put him on a pedestal. On the other hand, he *let* me. Some people who get put on pedestals *like* it there.

I see my mistake as giving up too much of myself when I met Charlie. In that way, I'm no different than millions of other women who lose themselves in their relationships. I didn't just partner with Charlie, *I fused* with Charlie, and when he left me I felt that I was nothing, invisible, dead. As I've said, it took me seven years to get "Harriett" back. I'm still working on it, even at this late date. It's a lifetime job.

From what I observed, Jill Ireland didn't have that *envelopment* problem that I had. Jill always seemed to know how to get her wants and needs met, whereas I was over forty before I even knew that I *had* any wants and needs. Maybe if I'd sent Charlie's shirts to the Chinese laundry the way Jill did, my whole life would have been different!

But as it has all turned out, I, too, in spite of the rough spots, am satisfied.

I know I loved Charlie. I know he loved me. We ended up disappointing each other. At the time, neither one of us could handle that disappointment. Had we known then what we know now -- had we each had more maturity and perspective -- maybe we would have survived it. We'll never know.

In July of 2003, Charlie, who had been ill with a number of conditions, was rushed to Cedars Sinai Hospital in Los Angeles. This occasioned one more big, tabloid-size drama in our lives and in the newspapers. Knowing that Charlie was dying, I wanted to visit him to say my final goodbyes. But Charlie's third wife, Kim, 36, another actress, said no. According to Tony, who was at Charlie's bedside (Charlie was barely conscious and not in on the discussion), Kim threw up her hands when Tony asked if his Mom could visit and said, "I *knew* this would happen! I *knew* this would happen!" I wrote her a letter pleading with her to be allowed to see Charlie, and Tony begged her on my behalf, but Kim refused my request. I never got to tell Charlie goodbye. That tore me up.

Charlie died on August 30th, 2003. He was buried in a hilltop grave in Vermont on Sept. 7, 2003. Tony and Suzanne were there.

Because I didn't get to say goodbye to him in person, I asked Tony to say something special from me at the funeral -- when he was alone.

After the funeral service was over and everyone had left, Tony went back to Charlie's casket and said:

> *"Every night before you and my mom went to sleep, you said this to her -- and now she has asked me to say it to you, through me: 'Sleep pretty; have pretty dreams, and remember I loved you very, very much.'"*

As of this writing, it has been sixty-four years since Charlie Buchinsky said those fateful words to me, *"C'mere,"* at the water fountain at the Bessie V. Hicks School of Stage, Screen and Radio.

Charlie was the love of my life, the foundation of my youth. I married him because of the man he was and I divorced him because of the man he became.

I never remarried.

In a rare philosophical moment immediately following the death of his brother, Dempsey, Charlie said to me, *"The only things in life that are permanent are memories."*

This is a poem that I've told my children I want to be read at my own funeral. It speaks to my feelings about love and loss:

*The longest day is in June, they say*
*The shortest in December*
*But it didn't come to me that way*
*As I remember*
*The shortest day you came to stay*
*And filled my life with laughter*
*The longest day you went away*
*The very next day after.*

-- Anonymous

The years went by so fast. It feels as though Charlie was in my life and I was in his for only an instant — and then he was gone.

# APPENDIX:
# MAGAZINE & TABLOID HAPPENINGS
# THROUGHOUT THE YEARS

public as "Mrs. **Charles Bronson**" ... and then, following her divorce, as the anonymous "Debra" on KABC Talkradio.

Now, due to her most recent role as author, Bronson has finally allowed her own identity to come into focus. Although she claims that talk radio is truly her "first love," she has found writing to be quite stimulating and considers herself an "idea girl."

Her first book, *Shut Up, I'm on the Phone!*, was published by Price/Stern/Sloane. Her second, *Do I Have a House for You!*, by the same publisher, is set to hit the bookstores in May. The author describes her upcoming book as "a satirical view of the real-estate scene. Without a sense of humor we could all go bananas!"

On a more serious note, Bronson has a novel in the works about a divorcée. When asked if it deals with her relationship to her hubbie, she politely insists she has no intention of writing about their marriage. However, she adds modestly that "it *was* very stimulating."

**Charlie's Ex-Angel Strikes Back**

"I like being *myself*," exclaims **Harriet Bronson**. Sound ironic? Well, it is, considering that for 16 years she was recognized by the

---

*LOS ANGELES* Magazine, April 1980

**Headline: Charlie's Ex-Angel Strikes Back** "'*I like being myself,' exclaims Harriett Bronson. Sound ironic? Well, it is, considering that for 16 years she was recognized by the public as 'Mrs. Charles Bronson' and then, following her divorce, as the anonymous 'Debra' on KABC Talkradio. Now, due to her most recent role as author, Bronson has finally allowed her own identity to come into focus. Although she claims that talk radio is truly her 'first love,' she has found writing to be quite stimulating and considers herself an 'idea girl.' Her first book*, titled, Shut Up, I'm on the Phone*, was published by Price/Stern/Sloane. Her second*, Do I Have a House for You! *by the same publisher, is soon set to hit the bookstores. The author describes the upcoming book as 'a satirical view of the real-estate scene. Without a sense of humor we could all go bananas!'*"

## Finally Taking "My Turn"
### March 6, 1987

*Los Angeles Herald Examiner Weekend Magazine*
**Headline: "Bronson Brightens the Graveyard Shift:** She Presides Over 5-Hour Talk Show,"
by Ray Richmond, *Herald* staff writer.

## 1989

ANOTHER WIFE'S NOTES

The first thing **Harriett Bronson, Charles** Bronson's wife from 1949 to 1965, wants you to know is that she is sympathetic toward her ex-husband's wife, Jill Ireland, and impressed by the courage that Ireland has shown in her latest bout with cancer. But Harriett is also extremely upset with the way she was portrayed in Ireland's recent book, *Life Lines.* Harriett feels that Jill painted her as a heartless mother in a hopelessly failed marriage. "I felt my marriage to Charlie was a good one until Jill came on the

them back. We went t court, and then the chi went back and forth. B Jill's book makes it loo I abandoned them." H ett is now talking to pu ers about her own boo *Hollywood and Bronson* land's spokesman says has no comment. •

IS NOTHING SACRED?

**Charlie Chaplin,** who w have turned 100 last m returns to life—sort of an animated figure in a week cartoon series fo dren on HBO called *C Chaplin's Little Tramp i*

Photo caption: Harriett Bronson, with Charles in 1959, is miffed the book by Jill Ireland, le

***PEOPLE* Magazine, May 1989, *"Take One"* by Pamela Lansden. *Photo Caption: "Harriett Bronson, here with Charles Bronson in 1959, is miffed at the book by Jill Ireland."***

What I was miffed about was the fact that in her book, Jill once again painted a picture of me as a bad mother and let people think she'd "raised" seven children when two of those children just happened to be mine -- and I'd raised them! Her words hurt.

A surprisingly nice article appeared in the December 21, 1999 issue of THE GLOBE, written by Joe Mullins, about our daughter Suzanne's Wedding.

I always wondered whatever became of my wedding band (as mentioned in this book) – maybe the same thing that happened to our marriage and to Charlie's life -- gone.

## 2002

Publicity Photo for A & E
Network's Biography:
Charles Bronson: Brute Force

Prometheus Entertainment and Foxstar
Productions in Association with
Fox Television Studios and A&E Network

Various articles and TV documentaries have appeared about Charlie, both before and after his death. Many of the writers and producers of these articles and shows have been very interested in my connection to him as his first wife, including those involved in the above A&E TV Biography called "Charles Bronson: Brute Force" (Foxstar Productions/ Van Ness Films, 2002). Charlie, then in the last year of his life, did not cooperate with the production. Instead, A&E used TV interviews that he had done elsewhere and inserted them into the show. Originally, I was just supposed to be one of the "interviews," but they liked what I did and I ended up actually narrating certain sections of the show. I value that show because it helps give Tony and Suzanne a better picture of their parents' marriage and lives together.          -- HB

## 2003
## The Last Big Tabloid Drama

*EXAMINER*  **September 2, 2003**
**Headline:  CHARLES   BRONSON   DEATHBED**
**DRAMA - Sub-Heading:** *"Wife Bars His Ex From*
*Hospital."* (I describe this episode in detail in the book
when Charlie's new wife, Kim, wouldn't allow me to
visit him in the hospital to say goodbye.)

# BRONSON'S FINAL HOURS

By Francesca Michael

'No one wanted to contemplate life after Charlie'

Bronson's first wife Harriett

A S SCREEN legend Charles Bronson lingered near death, his wife and children anguished over whether to switch off the machines keeping him alive.

Doctors at the famed Cedars-Sinai Medical Center explained that nothing could be done to save the 81-year-old movie tough guy.

But his children could not bear to just let him go, says a family insider.

"Charlie was a life force," explained his first wife Harriett, mother of his two oldest children, who was married to him for 16 years.

She told The EXAMINER: "A man with his lust and gift for life doesn't go without leaving a major effect on the people who loved him. No one wanted to contemplate life after Charlie."

Stricken by dementia three years ago, Bronson was rushed to the hospital on July 28 after suffering a toxic reaction to heart medication. His vocal cords were paralyzed, but the failing star let it be known that he wanted to live, if possible.

It was then discovered that he had cancer, which had spread into his collarbone and was invading the rest of his body.

A tracheotomy was performed to help his breathing and he was hooked up to a life-support system and kidney dialysis equipment, although nothing could be done to contain the cancer.

Doctors gave the dire forecast — that he could not survive for, at the most, more than a few weeks — to a family group made up of his third wife Kim, his daughter Suzanne, his second wife Jill Ireland's sons, Paul and Val McCallum, and Katrina Bronson, a friend's daughter who was raised by Bronson and Jill.

His son Tony was hooked up on a telephone line, while his daughter with Jill, Zuleika, was detained in Seattle with her baby Dempsey, whom she named after her dad's favorite brother.

After Kim later consulted with Tony, who is Bronson's only natural son, she agreed that they would let nature take its course.

With Bronson's sad decline, old-style Hollywood suffered one of its biggest losses — and finally put to rest one of its most notorious scandals.

Bronson wooed and won Jill Ireland from under the nose of her husband David McCallum in 1963. The men were making The Great Escape and Jill was visiting the location when she caught Bronson's eye.

Harriett was back in Los Angeles with Suzanne and Tony and knew nothing of the romance for months.

When she sensed that something was wrong in her marriage, she turned to Ireland for advice and was told: "Maybe he's seeing another woman."

A detective she hired to check up on Bronson eventually told her the shattering news.

He was, and it was Ireland. Although the two women once got embroiled in a kicking, scratching, bruising bloody fight, they later made up. And when Jill was stricken with breast cancer, Harriett nailed her and wished her a full recovery. It was not to be, and Jill died in 1990.

Bronson married once more, to Kim, in 1998, when he was 77 and she was 36. He wanted to be buried near the splendid estate they shared in Windsor, Vt.

As The EXAMINER reported in our September 2 issue, on Kim's instructions, Harriett, who is writing a book called Charlie And Me: Remembering Us, was not allowed to visit Bronson's bedside to say goodbye.

She told The EXAMINER: "His memory will live on, because his movies are highly respected all around the world. Also, he was a gifted artist, who painted wonderfully well.

"As for me, just before I filed for divorce from Charlie, we had a blazing row and I hurled my gold wedding band at him. He picked it up and put it into his pocket. It cost $42 when we bought it in Philadelphia in 1948 and was inscribed 'Forever and ever. Love Charlie.'

"I was told that Charlie had always kept it. Although I wasn't allowed to see him to say goodbye, I would be forever grateful if it could now be returned to me."

Charles Bronson and second wife Jill Ireland, who lost her battle with cancer in 1990

SEPTEMBER 16 2003 EXAMINER 17

**EXAMINER  September 16, 2003**

I was quoted in the above 2003 article: *"Charlie was a life force. A man with his lust and gift for life doesn't go without leaving a major impact on the people who loved him. No one wanted to contemplate life after Charlie."*

Today, as I read over these words, I still cannot believe that Charlie is dead -- but he does live on through our children, Suzanne and Tony, and for that I am grateful.

# 2003

# CHARLIE IS GONE – THE OBITS

When Charlie died, there were obituaries from all over the world. (Left) *The New York Times.* (Below) *The Los Angeles Times;* an AP article; (Bottom) a PEOPLE Magazine article.

### OBITUARIES

## Charles Bronson, 81, Dies; Played Tough Guy in Movies

### 'Death Wish' Star Charles Bronson Dies

**LOS ANGELES** – Charles Bronson, the grim-faced tough guy who built a European following before making his mark in the United States with action films including his "Death Wish" series, died Saturday of pneumonia.

He was 81.

## AN APPRECIATION

## Bronson's gifts: a glorious toughness and 'the right face at the right time'

**Tender as Nails**

# About the Author

Born in Philadelphia, Harriett Bronson went to a local drama school to become an actress and fulfill her dream of going on the New York stage. Instead, she met and married a fellow acting student (now known as Charles Bronson) and followed him to California. After sixteen years of marriage, two children and a high-profile divorce, Harriett once again found herself looking for a career. She considered getting back into acting, but serendipity intervened and she ended up as a radio talk show host for a total of 9 years -- first on KABC, and then on KIEV and KGIL. One reviewer dubbed her husky "purr" the "best female voice in radio." Harriett is also the author of two humor books, and for a number of years worked as a personal manager for songwriters and authors. She has two adult children and lives in Los Angeles. She can be contacted through:

Timberlake Press
Box 129
Woodland Hills, CA 91365
www.TimberlakePress.com

Milton Keynes UK
Ingram Content Group UK Ltd.
UKHW021258260524
443279UK00021B/249